From the Other to the Totally Other

American University Studies

Series VII
Theology and Religion
Vol. 44

PETER LANG
New York • Bern • Frankfurt am Main • Paris

Andrius Valevičius

From the Other to the Totally Other

The Religious Philosophy of Emmanuel Levinas

PETER LANG
New York • Bern • Frankfurt am Main • Paris

Library of Congress Cataloging-in-Publication Data

Valevičius, Andrius
 From the other to the totally other.
  (American university studies. Series VII,
 Theology and religion ; vol. 44)
  Bibliography: p.
  1. Lévinas, Emmanuel. I. Title. II. Series:
 American university studies. Series VII, Theology and
 religion ; v. 44.
 B2430.L484V35   1988   194   88-6756
 ISBN 0-8204-0647-3
 ISSN 0740-0446

CIP-Titelaufnahme der Deutschen Bibliothek

Valevičius, Andrius:
From the other to the totally other : the religious
philosophy of Emmanuel Levinas / Andrius
Valevičius. – New York; Bern; Frankfurt am
Main; Paris: Lang, 1988.
 (American University Studies: Ser. 7, Theology
 and Religion; Vol. 44)
 ISBN 0-8204-0647-3

NE: American University Studies / 07

© Peter Lang Publishing, Inc., New York 1988

All rights reserved.
Reprint or reproduction, even partially, in all forms such as microfilm,
xerography, microfiche, microcard, offset strictly prohibited.

Printed by Weihert-Druck GmbH, Darmstadt, West Germany

To the memory of
Antanas Maceina

CONTENTS

Foreword ix

Key to Abbreviations xi

Introduction 1

I. THE THOUGHT AND STYLISTICS OF EMMANUEL LEVINAS

1. Totality and Infinity 15
2. The Other in Idealism: Schelling and Hegel 21
3. The Other and the Idea of the Infinite 31
4. The Face of the Other — The Trace of the Other 41
5. Responsibility and Substitution of the One-for-the-Other and the Horizon of the Infinite 59
6. Language as Prayer 75

II. EMMANUEL LEVINAS IN PERSPECTIVE

7. An Excessive Ethics 85
8. Levinas' Critique of Martin Heidegger 93
9. The Other in Judaism: Reading Levinas Between the Lines .. 103
10. Ethics and Judaism, or the Numinous 119
11. Rosenzweig and Buber 135
12. From East to West. Levinas and Russian Thought 147

Conclusion 157

Selected Bibliography 167

Foreword

In contemporary Continental Philosophy there is no name today more popular than that of Emmanuel Levinas, and in France, especially since the death of Jean Paul Sartre, no thinker held in greater esteem. Emmanuel Levinas has already been the inspiration of two generations of French intellectuals. Yet in the English speaking world this complex and original thinker is little known, if at all. The purpose of the present work is to provide an English language introduction to the thought of Emmanuel Levinas.

This book differs from others already written about Levinas: it is a study of Levinas as a religious thinker. The philosophy of Levinas is seen within the broad perspective of nineteenth and twentieth century philosophies of religion, as well as within his Jewish and Eastern European heritage.

The author wishes to express his gratitude to Yolande Girard and John Hellman who encouraged this project, to Brian Walker and John Kilburn for helping to prepare the final manuscript and to Donna Krasowski for proofreading it.

Key to Abbreviations of Levinas's Texts

EI   *Ethique et infini*. Paris: Fayard, 1982.
DEHH   *En décourant l'existence avec Husserl et Heidegger*. 3d ed. Paris: J. Vrin, 1982.
DL   *Difficile liberté*. Paris: Albin Michel, 1963.
OBBE   *Otherwise Than Being or Beyond Essence*, trans. Alphonso Lingis (The Hague: Martinus Nijhoff, 1981).
QLT   *Quatre lectures talmudiques*. Paris: Les éditions de minuit, 1968.
TI   *Totality and Infinity*, trans. Alphonso Lingis (Pittsburgh: Dusquesne University Press, 1979).

Introduction

Emmanuel Levinas was born in Kaunas, Lithuania in 1906. Levinas writes about his life and formation in an essay called 'Signature' at the end of *Difficile Liberté,* a collection of essays on social, religious and political themes. He tells how during his childhood in Lithuania, his first formative influence came from the Hebrew Bible. Next it was the Russian classics: authors like Pushkin, Dostoyevsky and Tolstoy. Finally, there was the Russian revolution which he experienced in the Ukraine.

In 1923 Levinas went to France to continue his studies, where he had Charles Blondell and Halbwachs as teachers. Later he studied under such people as Jean Hering, Leon Brunschvig, Gabriel Marcel and Jean Wahl. He became friends with Maurice Blanchot. Levinas also attributes influence to the tradition of contemporary Jewish writers such as Martin Buber and Franz Rosenzeig.

The greatest influences in the philosophical formation of the young Levinas came from Husserl and Heidegger whose lectures he attended in Freiburg. "It is from Husserlian phenomenology that Levinas derives the rigourous and systematic methodological tools of inquiry which distinguish his thought from that of other religious thinkers whose rich and novel insights often lack sound philosophical foundations."[1] It was Levinas who first introduced Husserlian phenomenology to France with his translation of Husserl's *Cartesian Meditations* into French and with the publication of his doctoral thesis *The Theory of Intuition in the Phenomenology of Husserl* in 1930.

In 1939 at the outbreak of the second world war Levinas, who was by that time a French citizen, was drafted into the French army and was captured and detained in a German prisoner of war camp until the end of the war. When he was released he was once again able to return to his philosophical research. It was at this time that he discovered the Talmud and became a fervent reader and commentator on it.

We can classify Levinas as a Jewish thinker in roughly the same sense that was can classify Hegel as a Christian thinker.[2] Just as Hegel philosophized about sacred history, revelation, community and the trinity, so does Levinas, on occasion, philosophize about religious concepts such as creation ex nihilo, selection, law and prophecy. One may be tempted to classify Levinas as a theologian but Levinas does not see himself as 'doing theology'. It is true that his writings are inspired by Judaism and the Bible but even when handling religious themes he attempts to express them in philosophical terms.

Levinas protests against his being called a Jewish thinker, as to be so might be to approach philosophical problems with a pre-set order of concepts based solely on religious tradition; without any kind of philosophical exertion. "A philosophical truth cannot be based upon the authority of a (religious) verse... sometimes I search (for a proof) in ancient wisdom and I illustrate the point with (religious) verse, but I don't prove by verse."[3] Elsewhere he says, "One could say that biblical thought has, to some extent, influenced my ethical reading of the interhuman, whereas Greek thought has largely determined its philosophical expression in language."[4] Levinas says of himself, "plutôt que penseur juif, je suis un juif qui pense" (rather than a Jewish thinker, I am a Jew who thinks).[5]

Someone once called Levinas the Heidegger of the French language. This comparison could only be levelled against his style of writing since ontologically the two philosophies differ, Levinas's style and language are, for the most part, difficult, and rather vague. He often introduces ambiguities into his thought; for example he calls true religious practice 'atheism', and social responsibility 'anarchy.' He often employs new or unaccustomed names and concepts such as the "geste d'être," "le dans," "le non," "Signifiance," "feuillure," "essance," "de-ception," "désaisissement," "ab-solution."

As with Heidegger, many of Levinas's reflections appear to be expressed in poetic images rather than philosophical concepts:" "Etre en tant que laisser un trace, c'est passer, partir, s'absoudre." His discriptive ability seems at times almost inexhaustible. The later Levinas calls the self a hostage and describes subjectivity, or the self as besieged, attached, assailed, beleaguered, expelled, stripped, dislodged, exposed, denuded, and defeated. Or again it is a power which deploys, entrenches itself, steals away, retreats, can betray or be betrayed, can be extradited, deported, subjugated, and which gives in: or on the contrary, which liberates itself, holds fast, ensures, holds up, resists, it can also take on or come out of clandestine cover, be anarchical, in danger, invaded, up against a wall, vulnerable, exposed to insult and injury; it can order, command and submit, and so on.[6]

Levinas borrows many motifs from religious language. He writes about 'absolution,' 'liturgy,' 'diaconate,' 'visitation,' 'epiphany,' 'kerygma,' 'eschatology,' 'prophecy,' 'advent,' 'incarnation' and others. These words are not meant to be taken in a theological sense but nevertheless it is impossible not to make theological connections or to see their theological connotations despite their usage in a profane context.

At the heart of Levinas's thought is an ethics which contests contemporary thought. Modern philosophy has wrought havoc. The unity of truth, the unity of self, the unity of the world, indeed the very unity of reason itself has been undermined by various historical and political theories. "The humanism of the other man is the answer to the problem posed by the crisis of Western liberalism, inasmuch as Western philosophy has otherwise failed to find a humane alternative to the idealist tradition. Modern man is reduced to an object of sociology or psychoanalysis, a plaything of technology, a pawn of ideology."[7] Levinas challenges this current contemporary state of affairs with a theory based on the radical exteriority of the other person as encountered in the exceptional exigency of social life.

The ethics of Levinas is not a system of values, it does not advocate adhering to transcendent or historical laws or inner principles; it is based, rather, in man's relationship to infinite Being. Moral experience is not as much the perception of the Absolute as the enactment or fulfillment of this perception. Levinas speaks of ethics as an "optics" which means that ethics is a way of perceiving "sui generis" and not just a secondary specialized discipline belonging to ontology, cosmology or philosophical anthropology; ethics is a beyond Being. Ethics passes into philosophy as a an attempt to think the difference between Being and beyond Being.

Levinas wants to separate ontology from metaphysics and he does so by removing ontology from its privileged position. By having done so he is able to establish a bond between metaphysics and ethics. The interpretation of this relationship forms the substance of his work and thought. What he is attempting to do is to reverse traditional procedures and base metaphysics in ethics rather than developing an ethics upon pre-established metaphysical foundations. This he does by constructing upon the concept of alterity:

> Levinas argues that traditional Western philosophy, including the work of Husserl and Heidegger, sustains a distinction between the one and the other. In empirical systems this distinction is retained as real; in idealistic systems it is rejected as illusory. But, Levinas argues, whether real or illusory, the distinction is always made and always rests upon the presupposition that it is constituted by a consciousness which discriminates. But the very possibility of incorporating the one and the other into a single point of view compromises the radical alterity, the 'exteriority' of the other. Alterity which can be conjoined with or separated from the one by thought is not true alterity but part of what Levinas calls "the same". Radical otherness derives from a more primordial source. It can never be adequately thought for it lies beyond ontology. It is reflected in the world through the advent of other persons.[8]

When Heidegger speaks of Western philosophy in terms of "Seinsvergessenheit," similarly Levinas would describe Western philosophy as an "oubli de l'autre" or an "egologie."

Another "leitmotiv" of Levinas's thought is the "Idea of the Infinite." Levinas begins with Descartes: amongst all ideas, says Descartes, the idea of the infinite distinguishes itself in so far as the "ideatum" exceeds the "idea" and is more perfect. Although on the one hand the idea of the infinite does have a significant role to play within consciousness, on the other, it contradicts the basic laws of consciousness as formulated by classical phenomenology. These laws maintain that the thought or 'noese,' that cogitatum is none other than a correlate of the cognito. But, in the case of the Infinite things are different. Here we have to deal with another kind of intentionality which is directed towards that which it cannot grasp. As Levinas says, the "alterity of the Infinite is not cancelled by the thought that thinks it,"[9] so that when I come to the idea of the infinite, simultaneously I think more than I think. The Infinite is not contained within the idea of the infinite. The Infinite is the radically, absolutely other. The Infinite is separated from me, who thinks it and it is precisely this separation which is the primary indicator of its infinity. Therefore the idea of the infinite is not something placed in us; it does not arise from any structure of the self. It is experience in the most radical sense since we can never bring to it a structure of intentionality adequate to it. It is a genuine relation which what is other than ourselves. "We cannot reintegrate its alterity into the same. The thinker who has an Idea of the Infinite goes beyond himself, exceeds himself, is more than himself."[10]

Metaphysics should be understood in light of the Idea of the Infinite. In the act of trying to think the Infinite, he who is doing the thinking is subjected to a kind of expulsion; he is going beyond his own thinking. It is here that a certain "exterior" becomes apparent in objective knowledge which Levinas calls "metaphysical exteriority." "In this sense a philosophy of metaphysics, for Levinas, is one in which there is a turning towards (aspiration) radical exteriority which at the same time constitutes goodness and truth."[11]

With concepts (such as radical exteriority, the turning towards the other, the alterity of the other) Levinas approaches the divine. The phenomena of the other opens up the way to the holiness of God. Again and again Levinas speaks of the other and Other in ways not too easily distinguishable from one another: "God is in one sense the Other par excellence, the Other in as much as Other, the absolutely Other. To the contrary, my neighbour, my brother, man, is infinitely less other than the absolutely Other, and in a certain sense, more Other than God."[12] In any event, it is by way of alterity the the realm of the divine is revealed. The relation with God begins in the relation with other men. Over and over, Levinas emphasizes the social origin of the human encounter with God.

What makes Levinas's philosophy so fascinating is that he reintroduces the question of God into philosophical debate, but without talking very much about God. Even though his philosophy is inspired by Judaism both ancient and modern, the problem of God as a *specific* theme does not arise. Nevertheless upon reading Levinas the divine seems to be an underlying presence on every page. Levinas maintains that any "desire of the Infinite" which I may possess is not oriented toward the divine but rather toward the other. Although Levinas claims that he is a philosopher and not a theologian, his philosophy constantly brings the reader to the threshold of the divine.

The notion of God which one finds in the religious writings of Levinas is "religiously the most clear of notions, philosophically the most obscure."[13] The religious dimension of the concept of God is clear because it comes to us through revelation. Its philosophical dimension is much more obscure because it has to be worked out by reason. It does not, however, have to remain obscure because it is described in the Talmud. This is the proposition that Levinas wants to put forward as an alternative to idealism, and to ontological philosophies in general. To have the ethical situation of man as a point of departure means to renounce all theosophical attempts.[14]

Therefore, Levinas is against all forms of pious theosophy. He wants to purify the heavens of the divine images by showing that God's existence can neither be demonstrated by ontology nor described by anthropomorphisms. But he is also conscious of the fact that man needs to discover some kind of system which will give him an unalterable certainty with regards to the existence of God. This certainty should not be a projection and neither should it be beyond the possibilities of man. This certainty is contained in ethics.

The "Gottesbild" of Emmanuel Levinas is best summed up by his comment that; "the Infinite does not burn the eyes that are lifted to him."[15] The relation of man to the Absolute is an atheistic one, a God-lessness, a relation purified of the violence of the sacred. The Absolute is not the numinous, the ego which approaches Him is neither annihilated on contact nor transported outside of it. Transcendence is to be distinguished from a union with the transcendent by participation. Monotheism implies metaphysical atheism. The dimension of the divine opens forth from the human face. A relation with the transcendent free from all captivation by the transcendent is a social relation.

Levinas makes a distinction between the 'sacred' and the 'holy.' The sacred consists of attempting to elevate natural things to the level of the divine as a compensation for the fear of not being able to rationalize them. The holy is the desire for the Infinite. The sacred gives us magic, whereas the holy communicates to us the transcendent, it opens up the realm of the Infinite which is beyond exteriority. The refutation of the concept of the numinous as it is contained within the notion of the sacred leaves man solitary, without gods, without the divine. In this stage man runs the risk of being an atheist. Nevertheless, the risk has to be taken, because only by means of it does man elevate himself to the spiritual notion of the transcendent. True monotheism must meet the exigencies of atheism. "The atheism of the metaphysician means, positively, that our relation with the Metaphysical is an ethical behaviour and not theology, not a thematization, be it a knowledge by analogy of the attributes of God."[16]

Finally, God arises to his supreme and ultimate presence as correlative to the justice rendered unto men. It is impossible to directly comprehend God, not because our intelligence is limited, but because the relation with infinity respects the total transcendence of the Other without being bewitched by it, and because our possibility of welcoming Him in man goes further than the comprehension that thematizes and encompasses its object. It goes on to infinity:

> The comprehension of God taken as participation in his sacred life, an allegedly direct comprehension, is impossible, because nothing is more direct than the face to face, which is straightforwardness. A God invisible means not only a God unimaginable, but a God accessible in justice. Ethics is the spiritual optics.[17]

The breach that leads to God (the 'vision') coincides with the work of justice, the uprightness of the face to face, for there can be no knowledge of God separated from the relationship with men. "The Other is the very locus of metaphysical truth, and is indispensable for my relationship with God... The Other is not the incarnation of God, but precisely by his face, in which he is disincarnate, is the manifestation of the height in which God is revealed."[18]

Levinas's primary concern is religious. He makes no secret of his religiousness; he speaks of it openly. Yet many of his readers, attracted to his style of writing, pay little attention to this, the essence of his thought. Other readers are not interested in his religiousness: what interests them is his phenomenological architecture. They read him as one who examines a church or a temple from a purely aesthetic point of view, unconcerned and unreflective about what the building represents for those who built it and worship in it.

This book will examine different aspects of the philosophical writings of Emmanuel Levinas, both religious and philosophical in which he deals with the transition from the Other to the divine. To speak in very general terms the following essay could be considered an examination of Emmanuel Levinas' 'Philosophy of Religion' even though Levinas has never systematically treated the question of religion, having said; "We propose to call 'religion' the bond that is established between the same and the Other without constituting a totality."[19]

At the beginning of this introduction it was quoted that Levinas derived from Husserlian phenomenology, "the rigorous and systematic methodological tools of inquiry which distinguish his thought from that of other religious thinkers whose rich and novel insights often lack sound philosophical foundation." The methodology of this book is neither very rigourous nor exceptionally systematic and the Husserlian tools of inquiry have for the most part been left untouched. The author's intention has been to cast some light upon a few of the "rich and novel insights" in the writings of Emmanuel Levinas which we hope may some day themselves become sound philosophical foundations.

This book has been written in two parts. In Part I, "The Thought and Stylistics of Emmanuel Levinas," reproduces Levinas's 'philosophical style'; In Part II, "Emmanuel Levinas in Perspective," examines Levinas within a historical-philosophical context, in straightforward English. Roland Blum, in an excellent essay entitled "Emmanuel Levinas' Theory of Commitment", writes:

> ...it must be emphasized that Levinas' work presents special difficulties for the interpreter. His style is evocative rather than expository and his thought does not develop through a series of carefully reasoned arguments but rather by semi-poetic, rhapsodic and grammatically elusive meditations around certain central intuitions and metaphors. Any attempt to bring precision and clarity to his views is perhaps tantamount to their violation, but there seems to be no other way to gain leverage on his valuable but often opaque style of thought. Furthermore, his views are so anchored in a certain philosophical tradition, that of 19th and 20th century idealism, that a critical exposition of his philosophy involves to an unusual degree reference to the historical doctrines which influenced him.[20]

Levinas is a very complex writer and since his style of expression is so much an integral part of what he is trying to achieve it cannot be ignored, even in the face of an occasional lack of clarity, for lack of clarity is often the result he intends. This is because he is a religious writer of the continental tradition. Lack of clarity may repel analytical philosophers and the Anglo-Saxon mind, but it often attracts theologians, metaphysicians, mystics and other transcendentalists, all of whom have a much higher level of tolerance for ambiguity, since every entry into the realm of the religious is an entry into ambiguity. It is the sectarian mentality which seeks to remove the paradoxes from religion and give religion the guise of being 'scientific.' Paradox is that on which religion pivots, and also that which can make belief so difficult.

Another reason for the obscurity inherent in Levinas's writing is the linguistic milieu in which he writes and works — the French language. The 'esprit français' is, like religion, favourably disposed to paradox and ambiguity. Often the more complex and obscure a text, the more the French like it. One need only look at the popularity of contemporary French language intellectuals like Algirdas Greimas or Jacques Derrida to substantiate this. Perhaps it is best summed up by Blaise Pascal: "Qu'on ne nous reproche donc plus le manque de clarté puisque nous en faisons profession." (Let us not be reproached for lack of clarity seeing that we make a profession of it). This may seem like a strong and unjust accusation to make but it is one which does not apply to French alone. Conceptual patterns are definitely linked to language and each language, with its various syntactic and semantic possibilities, allows for a variety of expressions which are unique to that language, translated (if at all) with the utmost difficulty. German classics such as Hegel pose enormous problems for the translator, e.g. the phrase "aufgehoben und damit festgestellt" (released and thereby fixed into place). When philosophers wrote in Latin there was also no lack of expressions and compound words the meanings of which puzzle us today.

There is also the question of poetry or philosophy. Martin Heidegger said that his entire philosophy could be considered a commentary on Rilke's poetry and especially on the "Duineser Elegien."[21] When one examines the intellectual worlds of Heidegger and Rilke one sees obvious similarities. The difference is that Rilke expresses his thoughts by way of symbolistic images and Heidegger through abstract philosophical concepts. However, the inner creative "Geist" — the 'entelechie' of which Aristotle spoke — is the same: the same world, foreign and distant; the same human being, thrown (geworfen) out into existence; the same life charting a course towards death with no view of a beyond in sight. Whether or not Heidegger consciously appropriated Rilke's experiences and then set them to philosophical theory is a question that only Heidegger himself could answer. One thing is clear: Rilke's poetry and Heidegger's philosophy have their source in a common experience of life and grow out of a common 'Weltanschauung.'

There is a deep relationship between poetry and philosophy. To say that philosophy is the complete opposite of poetry is to speak of forms of expression, not inner essences. Both have words as their only medium of expression. Both the poet and the philosopher create by speaking — "Nec aliter quam dicendo facis," in the words of St. Augustine. It is by way of words that poetry and philosophy come to life. Their principal activity is in naming the qualities, relationships and essences which they see in things.

This is different from the naming activity of the scientist. Names for a scientist are usually only labels, attached to the surfaces of things. Thus science does not like words; it prefers formulas. Philosophy is no more a science than is poetry. Philosophy is an abstract and speculative activity. It does not possess the tools for exact verification of its hypotheses as do the natural sciences. Every philosopher, like every poet, interprets the world around him as he sees it. Neither possesses the ultimate truth. Each may say things that are true, but neither can give an all-encompassing explanation of how reality works. Nor can the scientist, for that matter, once he seeks to go beyond his "laws of nature."

The word as a creation is two-fold in nature. Firstly, the phonetic sounding of the word is associated with an image. This pictorial element of the word is usually its primordial meaning. The phonetics of a word, its pronunciation, may change over the course of time but the word retains, at least in part, its original meaning. The word does not contain this element in a material sense — that would be a form of magic — but it does contain the representation of reality.

Poetry seeks to illuminate this original impression of the word. In this sense poetry is not foreign to everyday speech; on the contrary, it draws upon everyday speech, seeking to unfold its primordiality.

As well as this pictorial meaning there is, secondly, a conceptual meaning, as every word contains not only the individual and concrete but also the abstract and generic. Whether the conceptual quality has always existed, from the very origin of any given word, is unknown. Yet it is true that the more 'civilized' a society becomes, the more abstract words become — the original 'weight' of the word is lost. In some societies words of love still equal the actions themselves in significance and importance. To speak such words vainly, without the intention of taking the consequential responsibility which they carry, is a moral transgression.

Philosophy illuminates the conceptual meaning of the word as poetry does the pictorial. Compared with everyday speech, philosophy can appear as obscure as poetry, but both draw upon everyday speech as their very source. Words form the bridge between philosophy and poetry.

In poetry words are used pictorially but never fully lose their conceptual quality; in philosophy words are used as concepts but also retain some of their pictorial element — the fermenting ground of both is everyday speech. There is a thin line between philosophy and poetry: resembling one another, when they have blended so closely and with such great genius that they can no longer be distinguished, we call it "The Dialogues of Plato."

Poetry, philosophy and everyday speech — in his own brilliant way Levinas draws upon and mixes all three under the influence of Heideggerian etymologies. This is why his style is so difficult to follow. If Heidegger's philosophy was Rilke's imagery translated into concepts, Levinas' philosophy is Old Testament imagery and poetry along with Judaic legendry so translated, blended with plays on words from Christian theology and Greek philosophy.

Notes:

[1] Edith Wyschogrod, *Emmanuel Levinas: The Problem of Ethical Metaphysics* (The Hague: Martinus Nijhoff, 1974), vi.
[2] Ibid.
[3] François Poirié, *Emmanuel Lévinas: Qui êtes-vous?* (Lyon: La Manufacture, 1987), 111.
[4] "Dialogue with Emmanuel Levinas," interview by Richard Kearney, in *Face to Face with Levinas*, ed. Richard Cohen (Albany: State University of New York Press, 1986), 21.
[5] Poirié, 13
[6] J. De Greef, "The Irreducible Alienation of the Self," in *The Self and the Other: The Irreducible Element in Man*, ed. Anna-Teresa Tymienicka (Boston: The Reidl Publishing Co., 1977), 27.
[7] Steven G. Smith, *The Argument to the Other: Reason Beyond Reason in the Thought of Karl Barth and Emmanuel Levinas* (Chico, California: Scolars Press, 1983), 197.
[8] Wyschogrod, viii.
[9] DEHH 172.
[10] Wyschogrod, 92.

[11] Stefan Strasser, *Jenseits von Sein und Zeit* (The Hague: Martinus Nijhoff, 1978), 10.

[12] QLT 36.

[13] QLT 71.

[14] Fernando Filioni, "Dio e l'alterità nel pensiero di Emmanuel Levinas," *Aquinas* 22 (1979): 32.

[15] TI 77.

[16] TI 78.

[17] TI 78.

[18] TI 40.

[19] TI 40.

[20] Roland Paul Blum, "Emmanuel Levinas's Theory of Commitment," *Philosophy and Phenomenological Research* 44 (1983): 146.

[21] H.F. Angeloz, *Rainer Maria Rilke* (Paris, 1936), 321.

PART I

The Thought and Stylistics of Emmanuel Levinas

1
Totality and Infinity

Although Emmanuel Levinas has published numerous books and articles on Judaism he is best known for three philosophical works: *The Theory of Intuition in the Phenomenology of Husserl*, *Totality and Infinity*, and *Otherwise than Being or Beyond Essence*. It is in the two latter books that Levinas's originality comes to full light and maturity.

In *Totality and Infinity*, the most fundamental experience that experience itself could subjectively consider is the experience of the Other, the "experience par excellence," Levinas wants to argue that just as in Cartesian thought the idea of the infinite "spills over" so too the Other is out of proportion to the power and freedom of the "I." Out of the disproportion between the Other and the I arises moral consciousness. Moral consciousness is not an experience of values but rather access to an exterior being and this exterior being "par excellence" is the Other. Moral consciousness is not a form of psychological consciousness but its condition. Levinas refers to moral consciousness as "droiture," and uprightness or a straightforwardness before the Other. It is when "I look without guile or evasion into the defenseless eyes of the Other, absolutely deprived of all protection."[1] The face of the Other questions my own happy spontaneity, my own joyful "force qui va." The crowd in *War and Peace* to which Count Rostopchin delivers Vereshchagin hesitates form committing violence when it sees his face reddening and turning pale. The crowd is taken up in a feeling of humanity pushed to the extreme. In the same way, the people remain silent at the end of *Boris Gudonov*, conscious of the crimes committed by those wielding power.

Totality and Infinity attempts to systematize such experiences and oppose them to philosophical thinking that "reduces the Other to the Self, multiplies him into the totality making autonomy his highest principle."² Levinas vigorously opposes totalitizing conceptions of history such as Hegel's. For Levinas there is a radical opposition between politics and religion. The former enslaves liberty by encompassing it within the 'Great All.' Religion on the other hand, which for Levinas is the metaphysical relationship with the Other, is based in respect and mutual aid even beyond need, submission and generosity.

The reduction of the Other to the Self within totality can only come about through violence, through oppression or war. Levinas speaks about an ontology of war which resembles many an ontology, when philosophers begin to speak in such terms as "Seinsmächtigkeit des Seienden," "Vermögen," "Vermöglichkeit," "Potenz," etc… In the same sense he refers to a self-affirmation which like the above concepts can only exist when based upon power. As Heraclitus has remarked, war is the essence of reality, so too, all that is real is violent, exercises violence and fends off violence. But the most brutal part of war is that it forces people to assume roles which are not their own. War alienates and does so precisely because of its totality. War imposes a structure upon life from which no one is exempted. Beings lose their identity as they "file into" the objective system of war. "The visage of Being that shows itself in war is fixed in the concept of totality, which dominates Western philosophy. Individuals are reduced to being bearers of forces that command them unbeknown to themselves."³

The moral consciousness can sustain the mocking gaze of the political man only if the certitude of peace outweighs the evidence of war. Such a certitude is not obtained by a simple play of antithesis.⁴

War is not a result of politics or socio-economics but has a metaphysical cause — the totalization of Being. The individual finds his meaning in the totality to which he belongs. The uniqueness of his presence is sacrificed to the future, because only the future of the whole has as its task the preservation of the meaning of life of the individual. That is why it is only the future of the totality which counts. Individuals are merely replaceable puppets of epic events which are planned and observed by politicians. Philosophy cannot be content with allowing this ontology of war to have the ultimate say in matters. Moral consciousness demands peace and the certainty that there is such a thing as peace which is stronger than all evidences of war.

Since Western ontology is responsible for a totalitarianism of war, the idea of peace can only be affirmed beyond this ontology. Beyond the totality of war a new relationship to Being has to be discovered; "The peace of empires issued from war rests on war. It does not restore to the alienated beings their lost identity. For that a primordial and original relation with Being is needed."[5] This is only possible from a point of departure which no longer belongs to this totality from an *eschaton*, or eschatology.

Eschatology is normally thought of as a theological teaching of the "end of things," the "end" of the world. In this sense as a teaching about the "end" it is understood chronologically, historically. This is not what Levinas has in mind. What he is seeking is a new relationship with Being that surpasses the objective totality of existents (étants as opposed to être):

> But, when reduced to the evidences (historical, etc...) eschatology would then already accept the ontology of totality issued from war. Its real import lies elsewhere. It does not introduce a teleological system into the totality; it does not consist in teaching the orientation of history. Eschatology institutes a relation with Being beyond the past and the present... It is a relationship with a surplus always exterior to the totality, as though the objective totality did not fill out the true measure of Being, as though another concept, the concept of infinity were needed to express this transcendence with regard to totality, non-encompassable within a totality and as primordial (originelle) as totality.[6]

This 'beyond' totality and objective experience is reflected within the totality and history of experience. "The eschatological, as the beyond of history, draws beings out of the jurisdiction of history and the future; it arouses them and calls them forth to their full responsibility."[7]

There is a judgement in eschatology, but it is not the Hegelian notion of judgement (die Weltgeschichte ist das Weltgericht). In eschatology history is submitted to a judgement not contained within history. The eschatological notion of judgement implies that beings have an identity "before" eternity, before the accomplishment of history, "before the fullness of time, while there is still time; it implies that beings exist in relationship, to be sure, but on the basis of themselves and not on the basis of totality."[8] In Hegel's rationalization of history, the judgement of history is anonymous. Judgement falls without the judged having been given a chance to speak. Individuals are judged and condemned as members of a nation, class, race or group; they are seen as cogs in the wheel of totality. The eschatological vision breaks with the totality of wars and empires in which the individual does not speak. It does not envisage the end of history within Being, understood as a totality, but institutes a relation with the 'Infinity of Being' which exceeds the totality: "The first 'vision' of eschatology (hereby distinguished from the revealed opinions of positive religions) reveals the very possibility of eschatology, that is, the breach of the totality, the possibility of a signification without a context."[9]

To restate the above in other words, Levinas is convinced that the meaning of life is not in history but in the "era" of inter-subjectivity which discloses a messianic "era." The encounter with the Infinite restores to man his own individuality which was effaced through totalization. Totalization is thus broken through by man's contact with the Infinite, and this contact occurs within his encounter with another person.

This is where ethics enters the picture and as already mentioned, takes on a new role. Ethics has nothing to do with a system of values, nor does it have its foundation in any theory of Being. Ethics is primarily based upon the relationship of man to infinite Being: "The experience of morality does not proceed from this vision (the eschatological vision) — it consummates this vision;' ethics is an optics. But it is a 'vision' without image, bereft of synoptic and totalizing objectifying virtues of vision, a relation or an intentionality of a wholly different type..."[12] The practical situation in which totality breaks up, where this "vision" takes place in the gleam of exteriority or in the transcendence is expressed by the term 'infinity.' This concept of infinity does not lead to the acceptance of any dogmatic content. The relation with infinity cannot be stated in terms of experience because infinity overflows the thought that thinks it. "Its very infinition is produced in this overflowing."[13]

Finally, the eschatological vision does not oppose the experience of totality in the name of personal egoism or salvation. To the objectivism of totality a subjectivity born of the eschatological vision is opposed;

> The idea of infinity delivers the subjectivity from the judgement of history, to declare it ready for judgement at every moment... called to participate in this judgement, impossible without it. The harsh law of war breaks up not against an impotent subjectivism cut off from being, but against the infinite, more objective than objectivity.[14]

Totality and Infinity goes on, through very thorough phenomenological research to show that subjectivity is founded in the idea of infinity: distinctions are made between the ideas of totality and infinity and it is shown how infinity is produced in the relationship with the Other.

Levinas also reflects on infinition, the mode of being of the idea of infinity. Infinity does not first exist and then reveal itself. Infinition is produced as revelation, as a positing of its idea in me, wherein the self, the 'I,' contains in itself what it can neither contain nor receive solely by virtue of its own identity. Subjectivity which realizes the astonishing feat of containing more than it is possible to contain is presented as welcoming the Other, as hospitality; in it the idea of infinity is consummated. The welcoming of the face and the work of justice are not interpretable in terms of disclosure. "Phenomenology is a method for philosophy, but phenomenology — the comprehension effected through a bringing to light — does not constitute the ultimate event of being itself."[15]

Notes:
[1] DL 409.
[2] DL 409.
[3] TI 21.
[4] TI 21.
[5] TI 22.
[6] TI 22.
[7] TI 23.
[8] TI 23.
[9] TI 23.
[10] TI 23.
[11] TI 25.
[12] TI 25.
[13] TI 28.

2
The Other in Idealism: Schelling and Hegel

Schelling's *System of Transcendental Idealism* is a system which begins with the I and proceeds to develop the continuous history of self-consciousness; "the philosophical system is primarily about selfhood and its conditions, and has the basic character of an act."[1] It is a system which attempts to attain a comprehensive knowledge, to discover a principle whereby human knowing is determined. In knowledge itself, subject and object are united, are identical. But in order to explain this identity it must be thought away, and there are two ways of doing this:

> Either we can start with the objective and proceed towards the subjective, asking how unconscious Nature comes to be represented. Or we can start with the subjective and proceed towards the objective, asking how an object comes to exist for the subject. In the first case we develop the philosophy of Nature, showing how Nature develops the conditions for its own self-reflection on the subjective level. In the second case we develop the system of transcendental idealism, showing how the ultimate immanent principle of consciousness produces the objective world as the condition of the attainment of self-consciousness.[2]

Schelling understood these two lines of development as being complimentary to each other. "Schelling's conviction that the mutually complementary characters of the philosophy of Nature and the system of transcendental idealism manifest the nature of the Absolute as identity of subject and object, of the ideal and the real."[3]

If transcendental idealism is a "comprehensive knowledge," the question of the source of this knowledge arises. Schelling claims that it begins with the 'ego,' with the 'I.' "This must be accepted if anything else is to be certain. That there are things outside us will therefore only be certain for the transcendental philosopher in virtue of its identity with the proposition I exist."[4] This identity within the sphere of knowledge is self-consciousness, and self-consciousness is described by Schelling as the I; as knowledge of ourselves; as primary knowledge. Schelling elaborates: 'it is a kind of knowing for which there is no higher for humans, it always remains the first principle and it is a knowing of which we never get beyond.' In other words, it is the I which is the universally mediating factor in our knowledge, which is the ultimate principle of our knowledge.

The I is the absolute act with which all knowledge begins. The I exists through knowing itself and this act of self-knowledge is what Schelling calls intellectual intuition. It is the potential of the I to reflect upon itself: "the I is qualified as an intellectual intuition, it is differentiated from the empirical in as much as it produces its own object."[5] Hence intellectual intuition and the production of the object of transcendental thought are one and the same, and a system of transcendental idealism is basically a production or a construction of self-consciousness. The I is, much in the Fichtean sense, an unlimited act of activity. In order to become its own object, through intellectual intuition, it must limit this unlimited, predominant self-activity by setting something over against itself — namely, the not-I. The postulation of the existence of the not-I stems from the very condition of self-consciousness, the self's becoming conscious of itself — which, according to Schelling, is a process of which the self is unconscious. This process of production of the not-I must be unconscious because it is otherwise not possible to account for its existence within the framework of idealism. As Schelling maintains, "The Science of Knowledge cannot proceed from anything objective."[6] In this sense the unlimited activity of the I has to remain limited, but this limitation of the unlimited is itself limited, because it is transcended once the I presupposes Nature — the not-I.

Having laid the foundations for his *System of Transcendental Idealism*, Schelling goes on to treat the history of consciousness through various epochs, from primitive sensation to productive intuition, from productive intuition to reflection (the I being here conscious on the level of sense), and from reflection to the act of absolute abstraction, "by which the I reflectively differentiates itself from the object or not-I as such and recognizes itself as intelligence. It has become object to itself."[7] Thus one arrives at the second or practical part of transcendental idealism, wherein the I becomes an active and free power, and act of the self-determining will. Only as such is absolute abstraction explicable, as Schelling postulates in the first proposition of part four of the *System of Transcendental Idealism*; "First Proposition: Absolute abstraction, i.e., the beginning of consciousness, is explicable only through a self-determining, or an act of the intelligence upon itself."[8] The explanation of intelligence, and even knowledge, must be sought in the will. Intelligence is never purely theoretically based, and knowledge does not come through a passive apprehending of a world in which objects work upon the intelligence in a purely external or mechanical way. Intelligence and knowledge are only explainable "by supposing an absolute power of self-determination which is utterly independent of any act of mere knowing."[9] The self is not simply one of the many objects of knowledge, not simply a part of nature, but rather a pure self-activity which is the condition of the knowledge of Nature.

Intelligence is practical intelligence which has a conscious self-determination as its essence. This transition to practical philosophy creates problems for the idealist, and is the point where we become aware of the *other person*, who is brought in by the necessity of becoming conscious of ourselves. Schelling introduces his second proposition thus;

> The act of self-determination of the free action of the intelligence upon itself, can be explained only by the determinate actions of an intelligence external to it... First, then, we see at all events that a determinate action of an extraneous intelligence is the necessary condition of the act of self-determination, and thereby of consciousness; but we do not see how, and in what manner such an external act could be even the indirect ground of a free self-determination in ourselves. And secondly, we do not perceive how there can be any external influence at all upon the intelligence, and so also do not see how the influence of another intelligence upon it may be possible.[10]

The answer to this problem begins with the fact that there are a number of finite intelligences, each possessed of an external world and independent of the others, each in accordance with its peculiar will, which creates individuality. The dogmatist has knowledge of other finite intelligences and explains the limitation of the will of each in terms of their interaction with each other; he believes that individuality is determined by factors external to it. The idealist maintains the opposite — that he can know nothing which lies outside of his thinking activity, and that he can do nothing which is not in relation to his practical activity; no other intelligence can act upon him except in so far as he acts upon himself. How then does he know that there are other intelligences and do they in any way whatsoever act upon him? The answer is that in willing he finds himself limited to certain ends. In the consciousness of that limitation, he finds himself conscious of himself as an individual, and as an individual in relation to other selves.

> To achieve the original self-intuition of my own free activity, this latter can be posited only quantitatively, that is under restrictions; and since the activity is free and conscious, these restrictions are possible only through intelligences upon me, I discern nothing save the original bounds of my own individuality and would have to intuit these, even if in fact there were no other intelligences beyond myself. That although other intelligences are posited in me only through negation, I nevertheless must acknowledge them as existing independently of me, will surprise nobody who reflects that this relationship is a completely reciprocal one, and that no rational being can substantiate itself as such, save by the recognition of others as such.[11]

These other selves do not act upon him, since no intelligence can act upon another intelligence, but there is an indirect relation of different intelligences to another, as Schelling explains: "That an immediate influencing among intelligences is impossible, according to the principles of transcendental idealism, stand in no need of proof, nor has any other philosophy rendered such an influence intelligible. Hence nothing remains but to suppose an indirect influence between different intelligences..."[12] This relationship of different intelligences is referred to by Schelling as a "pre-established harmony." It is true that the world of nature exists only in relation to one's knowledge, but this does not exclude the possibility of the world being essentially the same to other intelligences. Apart from all the peculiarities of each individual there is a 'common world' — the world of natural science, of objects acting and interacting in space and time. In this common world there is also the constant interaction of intelligences, each conscious of its own acts and of its representations of the acts of others, each acting upon every other in and through their respective representations of each other's acts. Thus they ensure each other's freedom simultaneously, limiting each other in an indirect fashion, instead of through direct compulsion: "The never ceasing interaction of rational beings, regardless of their ever-increasing freedom, is thus alone made possible by what we call diversity of talents and characteristics, which, for that very reason, however much it may seem opposed to the drive for freedom, is itself necessary as a condition of consciousness."[13]

The consistency of the philosophy of transcendental idealism, wherein the objective world is basically the subjective which has become an object to itself, lies in that of the subject's relation to other subjects, since this is the condition of his knowledge of the objective and consequently of himself: "Only by the fact that there are intelligences outside me, does the world as such become objective to me."[14] A single individual alone by himself would not only not become conscious of his own freedom, but he would not even become conscious of an objective world — the other is necessary for one's own self-realization.

Later on, in Part Four of the *System of Transcendental Idealism*, Schelling expands upon the reality and the concrete action of the self-determining I under the conceptions of freedom, rights, the state and history. Here too the idea of the awareness of another intelligence — the other person — surface occasionally, affirming the free self-realization between individuals as the basis of freedom, the imperative morality, the measure in law-making and the realization of the substance of history: "History is thus a continual advance towards a pre-determined goal... realized in and through the will of individuals... a perfect state of which all men shall be citizens."[15] All the activities of the self-acting, self-determining selves must somehow be reconciled, brought into harmony. The I should will nothing else but self-determination; "This demand is nothing else but the categorical imperative or the moral law which Kant expresses in this way: you ought to will only that which other intelligences can will. But that which all intelligences can will is only pure self-determination, pure conformity to law. Through the law of morality, therefore, pure self-determination ... becomes an object for the ego."[16] Systems of Rights and the State are then deduced as conditions for moral action; history, realized within all these ideals, is a continuous unfolding of the Absolute, a continuous revelation. Schelling says, "there lies in the concept of history the concept of endless progress."[17]

Hegel's *Phenomenology of Spirit*, which has been described as the history of consciousness, is the study of the mind as related to an object. In this sense phenomenology would be the science of consciousness. Fichte and Schelling understood subjectivity to be the centre of life, but they understood it in a way which created a dichotomy between man and the world Spirit — opposed to Nature, God opposed the Nature, the infinite opposed to the finite. The Greeks had seen themselves as part of the whole: when they looked at themselves they also saw the world. This is the kind of harmony to be desired, the kind which Hegel seeks to restore by exposing the inherent contradictions of the understanding: The truth of the finite is to finish (die Wahrheit des Endlichen besteht darin zu enden) and what I opine is merely mine (Meinungen sind nur das meinige). Philosophy is concerned with truth. The subject must think the truth. Nature is rational — this the philosopher pre-establishes. Therefore human history must also be rational. The real is rational and the rational is real. Spirit means essentially the recognition of reason in others, the recognition that reason is real and that the real is reason. God is the absolute reason. But, there are the dichotomies, there is the disorder. Therefore, man seeks to perceive an order in every disorder. Man discovers reason everywhere. However in order to do so he must first himself be reasonable (vernunftig). In order to be reasonable himself he has to see others as reasonable. He discovers order in the world, he discovers the Spirit.

The *Phenomenology of Spirit* is basically a presentation of self-revealing knowledge. It is a way of purification. It can be divided into three main parts: 1) The first phase is the consciousness of the object as a sensible thing standing over against the subject. Here science is to be recognized as a phenomenon amongst others. It is the phase which Hegel names 'consciousness' (Bewusstsein). Simply put, it is when I reflect. It is where the adventure begins. 2) The second phase is 'self-consciousness' (Selbstbewusstsein). Knowledge is now a phenomenon of truth and the subject must decipher what is going on with him — or, more precisely, within him. Now I reflect that I reflect. The self-conscious consciousness is the consciousness which lives through the adventure. 3) The third phase is that of reason (Vernunft), which is represented as the synthesis or unity of the preceding phases on a higher level. In other words, the synthesis of objectivity and subjectivity. It is that I reflect upon the reflection and that I reflect upon the reflection of the reflection. Here knowledge is the highest phenomenon. It is absolute knowledge. Here philosophy is finally what it should be: science (Wissenschaft), and not just love of wisdom. The mind in this process proceeds from level to level.

Hegel begins with what he calls sense certainty — the uncritical apprehension by the senses of particular objects, to the naïve consciousness the most certain and basic form of knowledge, and also the richest. However, when the mind seeks to define what it knows, it can only come up with very general terms, suitable to a variety of objects. It does not really "know": a discrepancy has already arisen between the thing-in-itself (an sich) and what it is for me (für mich). This is where consciousness begins to make a distinction between knowledge and truth. What I considered to be a being-in-itself could only have been a being-in-itself for me — or so it seemed to me. I can only know a being-in-itself (an sich), but what I cognize is a being-in-itself for me, and only as long as it remains an in-itself for me (Identity-in-difference). Hence I can only look and see. I can, of course, try to pin the object down by the use of words such as 'here' and 'now,' but a moment later the words apply to another object. For example, I say that the Now *is*: immediately this Now becomes a Now that *was* — this Now is not, but rather was. But as a Was it is not. Therefore the Now was — as a Was. The Now is not, because there is only the Was, but the Was also is not, because it was. Hence, the Now is — but now it is a conceptual (gedachtes) Now, now bringing me further than I was a few sentences back, talking about the mere empirical Now. Slowly a development of consciousness is taking place — experience changes the experiencer. By such a means knowing begins to change, and the being-in-itself as well — the former being-in-itself is no longer there. I see too that consciousness, which Hegel calls natural (natürliches), is not as natural as it thinks itself to be. I begin to see that true cognition, in order to be so, must encompass the whole (das Ganze) — i.e., not only the sensible Now, but also the concept of the Now. The sensible fades away; only the conceptual remains. The finite always finishes (das Endliche endet); it passes into the horizon of the infinite — otherwise I couldn't speak of the finite. There is, therefore no real Now without the conceptual Now. I begin to see that when I run up against a limit I have already gone beyond it (hinaus), although it still remains a limit above and beyond which I cannot go (heraus). When I bump up against my finitude I trip into infinity, though remaining finite: knowing myself to be finite means knowing about the existence of an infinite. Consciousness has now been elevated above the level of sense-objects. What is to become of it?

In the *Phenomenology of Spirit* a conceptual development takes place, a development of perceptions and qualities, scientific understanding, meta-phenomenal or unobservable entities, hidden forces, and the idea of laws;

"In the end the mind sees that the whole realm of the metaphenomenal which has been invoked to explain sense-phenomena is the product of the understanding itself. Consciousness is thus turned back on itself as the reality behind the veil of phenomena and becomes self-consciousness."[18] Consciousness finally comes to the realization that the suprasensible world only really makes sense in relation to another suprasensible world: the being-of-itself of the world is essentially its being-for-another, for consciousness, the being-in-the-world of which is essentially a having-to-do-with-the-world. Consciousness is achieved by the turning of the objective world back upon itself, as a-being-aware-of-self (Selbstbewusstsein).

A strong idealistic turn or leap to self-consciousness has been carried out. Consciousness has now realized that in dealing with the world, under whichever laws, it is after all only dealing with a projection of itself: "and the world, on its side, becomes a manifold transfused with the intellective life of consciousness."[19]

Hegel begins with self-consciousness in the form of Desire (Begierde). Through Desire we become self-conscious. The subject in his contemplation of any certain 'thing' can become so absorbed that he even forgets himself. The more conscious he is of this thing, the less he is of himself. But as soon as he conceives Desire for the thing he is 'brought back to himself.' A man is hungry; he wants to eat: when he becomes aware of this, he also becomes aware of himself. Hence it is not a passive self-contemplation at the bottom of self-consciousness, but rather Desire. Consciousness comes to self consciousness out of a desire for complete conscious unity with the Other, a stage in the abstract dialectical development of consciousness. Self-consciousness seeks a reflection of itself in the external world and can find such a reflection only in another individual. If the self-consciousness were to be isolated in itself, it would be no more that an abstract awareness gathering up objectivity within itself: there would be only one kind of awareness taking place, that of the self being aware. In order to be more aware, the self requires a doubling of itself — the self can become its own object only if there are other selves in its field of objects: "The unity of self-consciousness must be at the same time a multiplicity of self-consciousness, or it is nothing at all; the multiplicity of selves must recognize each other as selves, or there is no unity at all."[20]

The Other is essential for self-consciousness. Man can arrive at self-consciousness only in the consciousness of another self and in mutual recognition (sich anerkennen). This is to recognize the Other in that he recognizes me: it is a social or 'we' consciousness. One arrives at self-consciousness when an 'I' becomes a 'We,' an I which is We and a We which is an I: two individuals encounter one another and must prove themselves to be Spirit in freedom to each other. They each recognize themselves as being recognized. This is identity in difference: the Other becomes the communal (das Allgemeine). Thus an action of a self is always determined through the action of another. The equality of I equals I. At first, each recognizes himself as individuated, but not once he recognizes the individuation of the Other: they are now individuated together — that is their communal. When can say "I am you and you are I" or "I that is me and me that is you," a reconciling "yes" is spoken and the union of selves is realized. Each one of us has two generalities, the individual and the universal, the generality of the communal; in our individuality we have access to the universal, and in the universal we discover our individuality:

> Thus unlike the Husserlian phenomenology of intersubjectivity which first discovers the self and then seeks to "constitute" a world of selves, the Hegelian phenomenology finds that other selves are essential to the discovery of one's own self and that the 'discovery' is actually a producing of oneself in relation to others.[21]

Only in a community of selves is self-consciousness possible.

Levinas calls these notions of the Other a totality. The self and the Other are both approached on the self's own terms; both belong to one total system of explanation. Yet despite the necessity of the Other for the self's self-discovery, Levinas says that the priority given to the self is a denial of the Other. He wants to see the Other as a priority, approached on its own terms. The relationship with the Other is not one of symmetry or equality. The Other always comes first.

Notes:
[1] Michael Vater, introduction to J.W.F. Schelling, *System of Transcendental Idealism (1800)*, trans. Peter Heath (Charlottesville: University of Virginia Press, 1978), xxx.

2. Frederick Copleston, *A History of Philosophy*, vol. 7, Part I (Garden City, New York: Image Books, 1965), 144.
3. Ibid.
4. Schelling, 8.
5. Ingtraud Görland, *Die Entwicklung der Frühphilosophie Schellings in der Auseinandersetzung mit Fichte* (Frankfurt am Main: Vittorio Klosterman, 1973), 177.
6. Schelling, op. cit.
7. Copleston, 145.
8. Schelling, 161.
9. John Watson, *Schelling's Transcendental Idealism* (Chicago: S.C.Griggs & Co., 1882), 153.
10. Schelling, 161.
11. Ibid., 169.
12. Ibid., 163.
13. Ibid., 170.
14. Ibid., 173
15. Watson, 178.
16. Copleston, 146.
17. Ibid., 147.
18. Ibid., 221.
19. Howard P. Kainz, *Hegel's Phenomenology Part I: Analysis and Commentary* (Alabama: University of Alabama Press, 1976), 83.
20. Quentin Lauer, *A Reading of Hegel's Phenomenology of Spirit* (New York: Fordham University Press, 1976), 103.
21. Ibid., 101.

3
The Other and the Idea of the Infinite

Levinas's reflections on the Other resemble those of Hegel, in whose *Phenomenology of Spirit* the self can only discover itself by way of other selves. For Levinas, the self is completed and constructed through the revelation of the Other. Even though Levinas seems to accept the basic assumptions of idealism, he rethinks and reforms them, in order to focus on the priority of the Other, his main concern. This he does by insisting upon the self's inability to constitute the Other's consciousness as experienced by the Other. It is, then, precisely this inability of the self which gives the Other in his otherness meaning for the self. At first this appears to be a solipsism: "What I constitute... is my inability to constitute." Husserl tried to escape this solipsism by suggesting that this inability is precisely what we constitute as the existence of the Other. Levinas tries to escape it by insisting on the priority of the Other, raising its status nearly to that of an 'other worldliness.' Roland Blum explains:

> Levinas's basic... problem is that he remains too indebted to the very system he rejects. He is unconcerned about a doctrine of nature and appears to hold no theory of genuine external relations among persons... As a result, any relation to another person becomes my experience of my relation to that person; this in turn makes the Other into a mere feature of my experience unless there is some way to avoid the implicit solipsism.... If the Other is not to remain a mere feature of my consciousness, he must originate independently of my world, in a way analogous to God.[1]

Levinas maintains that there is a truth which the ego can know and a truth which lies beyond the everyday world that is vulnerable to the reductive powers of the ego. Philosophy itself points the way to this truth for it seeks that which transcends the everyday. Philosophy properly understood, according to Levinas, is metaphysics, an inquiry into the question of the divine.[2] Levinas does not mean that the object of our inquiry exists because we inquire about it, but perhaps more in the way of the following; when we inquire into the truth, we want more than the results of our inquiry, for these results can only be expressed in categories already familiar to us. Philosophy is a quest for heteronomy; but the Other will not be found to be analytically contained in our idea of him. Levinas does not reinstate the ontological argument. Rather he believes that we will find the Other, whom we seek, in the sphere of intersubjectivity, and that the alterity we find will always exceed the idea we can have of the Other. Furthermore:

> ...it is the nature of man to be a 'taught' being. Teaching is the distinguishing factor of exteriority which penetrates through to me. God himself teaches me by means of revelation. It is not true that man's spirit develops all by itself and that knowledge is basically a recalling of an already pre-established interiority. 'I am taught' which means that truth comes from beyond. Being 'taught' means the infinite of exteriority. One can also say that to think is to have the idea of the infinite, or to be taught.[3]

Philosophy looks for the truth and does so through experience and in freedom. In truth, the thinker has a relation to a reality, distinct from himself, other than himself, "absolutely other," according to Jankelevitch. In order to be worthy of the name, experience has to take us beyond the nature of things in which we find ourselves. Plato had said that truth would come as a result of a movement beginning in the familiar, known, world and moving towards a foreign world, towards a "là-bas." For Plato truth implies transcendence rather than just exteriority, pointing towards the dimensions of the ideal where philosophy becomes metaphysics and metaphysics investigates the divine.

However truth can also mean free adherence to a proposition based on the results of free research by a researcher or thinker who is not being pressured by any constraints, and thus expresses himself in truth. "But what is the truth if none other than a refusal on the part of the thinker to alienate himself in the adhesion, if none other than the conservation of his own nature, of his own identity, if none other than the fact to remain the same regardless of the all of the unknown lands into which thought seems to lead him."[4] Philosophy essentially attempts to reduce everything to the same, to show the fundamental same-ness of all that seems to be. Philosophy seeks an autonomy where there is no longer anything irreducible, which could put a limit on thinking and defines such "unlimited" thinking as freedom. This is man's conquest of Being through reason. Liberty and autonomy are equivalent to the reduction of the Other to the Same. All of the above would not represent some sort of abstract schema but the human I. The I would unfold as the identifying of diversity. Regardless of all that happens, of all the years that go by, the I remains the same. The I remains the same in making its own history. This is the outcome of Western philosophy which likes to support itself upon freedom and familiarity. Seen from such a position it would seem that Western philosophy has excluded the transcendent. All that is other is seen to be contained within the Same; only then can philosophy be seen as autonomous.

Levinas calls this type of autonomous philosophy wherein freedom is sure of its rights and works for its own self-affirmation, 'narcissism.' Anything foreign entering this philosophy of autonomy is seen as an obstacle, something to be either integrated or surpassed. It is then this victory of the I over the foreign or Other which constitutes truth in Western thought. As Levinas describes it, in Western thought freedom triumphs only when the soul arrives at universality, and encompasses the totality of Being. All of experience, the world, the elements and objects, everything must become part of the dialectic of the soul speaking to itself.[5]

In Western thought the essence of truth does not lie in a relation with an unknown God, but rather in the already known which has to be discovered, or freely constructed within oneself. This kind of truth is strongly opposed to a vision of a God of revelation. Philosophy so seen, is what Levinas calls an 'atheism' or 'irreligion,' a philosophy which denies a self-revealing God and puts truth in humankind. In this 'atheism' everything introduced or taught to the soul was already contained within the soul, the marvelously autarchic 'I' which leads all philosophy to become an egology. Truth is reduced to something dependent upon a free movement within the I which rules over all.

Next, the question of the not-I arises. In order to understand the not-I the alterity of the Other is reduced to an abstraction, to a neuter. Instead of seeing him in his remarkable singularity he becomes to us a theme and an object. He becomes categorized in a file of ideas. Instead of attempting to comprehend the unique individual, who exists in his singularity, we see him in his generality.

This is where the philosophy of autonomy begins to show similarities with a philosophy of power and violence. The significance of things exterior to my personal human liberty in their generality does not mean merely an innocent comprehension of them; it is also a domestication and a possession of them. This does not deny the reality of the Other but rather his independence. "In a civilization marked by a philosophy of the Self, freedom is a richness. Reason which appropriates the Other is a power."[6]

Levinas maintains that this supremacy of the Self over the Other is still to be found in the philosophy of Heidegger. When Heidegger outlines the way of access to all singularities he does so by way of Being, which itself is not a particular Being or a gender in which all other particularities are contained, but rather the act of being itself as expressed by Being as a verb and not as a noun; "Levinas interprets Heidegger as having correctly understood being as the power of Being,"[7] Heidegger brings us to singularity by way of a neuter which renders thought intelligible. When Heidegger sees man possessed by freedom rather than man possessing it, he places man under the neuter which enlightens freedom without putting it into question and in this sense Heidegger is perfectly in tune with the current of Western philosophy.

Furthermore, Levinas interprets Heidegger's work as an exaltation of the already present anti-religious tendencies in Western thought. For Levinas, Heideggerian atheism is paganism; it predates the Socratic world view for it is rooted in pre-Socratic texts and it is thereby anti-biblical. Heidegger shows, 'in what drunkenness the clear sobriety of the philosopher bathes.'

Because freedom in Heidegger is illuminated only under the concept of Being, it is not essential. It is obedient to Being, but it is not a freedom which is much examined, it is not put into question nor is it conscious of its injustices. "Being is inseparable from the comprehension of Being, Being is already the invocation of subjectivity. But Being *is not* an existent (étant)."[8] The neuter regulates thoughts and beings. Man's consciousness of his finiteness does not come to him from the idea of an infinite, and is not seen as an imperfection: "Heidegger's philosophy is precisely none other than weakness and fault towards oneself — the product of a long tradition of proud heroism, of dominance and of cruelty."⁹ Heidegger subordinates the relation with the Other to the relation with neuter Being, and thereby continues to exalt the will to power in which the Other can only disturb my conscience.

Levinas criticizes Heidegger's thoughts on Being's having been forgotten by different realities which themselves are illuminated by Being. Heidegger blames philosophy after Socrates for this and bewails the orientation of intelligence towards technology. Levinas, however, says that the view of power maintained by Heidegger is much less humane than any sort of technology. For Heidegger existence means accepting as natural that man receives his meaning from his environmental setting, from his "Sitz im Leben." Levinas sees this as a pagan viewpoint. He says that Heidegger's philosophy is essentially anti-religious because it is a religion the wrong way around (religion à rebours):

> In short, the well known hypothesis of Heidegger's philosophy; the supremacy of Being over being, of ontology over metaphysics continues to affirm the Self's dominating over the Other wherein freedom even if identical to reason, precedes justice. But this last term, justice, does this not mean giving precedence to the Other and his needs before the Self?¹⁰

Levinas wants to continue a philosophical tradition which is just as ancient as that of Heidegger, but one which is not based on the reductive power of the Self. He says, contrary to Heideggerians and neo-Hegelians for whom philosophy begins as an atheism, the tradition of the Other is not necessarily religious, it is philosophical. Plato shows himself to be in this tradition in *Phaedro*, where he places the Good beyond being and says that true discourse is talking with the Gods.

Levinas builds his philosophy of the Other upon an analysis of Descartes's Idea of the Infinite. According to Descartes, the thinking I stands in a relation with the Infinite. This relationship does not unite the 'I' which contains with the content, (le contenant au contenu) because the 'I' cannot contain the Infinite. Neither does it unite the content to the 'I' which contains (the one containing) because the I is separated from the Infinite. The relation, negatively described, is the "Idea of the Infinite" in us.

We have ideas of many things but the Idea of the Infinite is exceptional in the sense that its "ideatum" surpasses its idea. As mentioned in the introduction, with the relation of an 'I' to the Infinite we have to deal with another kind of intentionality, one which is directed towards that which it cannot grasp. The Infinite is not contained within the Idea of the Infinite; it is a radical and absolute Other and Levinas maintains that this idea has been put into us, it is not a reminiscence. The experience with the Other is an experience with exteriority, without the possibility of integrating this exteriority to the Self, and this experience of the Idea of the Infinite is realized within social relations.

This relation consists in our approaching a Being who is absolutely exterior. The infinitude of this Being, which cannot be contained within our ideas guarantees this exteriority. It is not simply a question of distance between subject and object. The object is not a problem for us since we know how to integrate it into the identity of the Self. "The I makes of the infinity of the exterior by its theme, its property, its plunder, its prey or its victim. The exteriority of the infinite Being manifests itself in an absolute resistance which from the moment of its apparition, of its epiphany, it opposes to all of my powers."[11] In a beautiful description of the way the Other opposes my powers and of how the Infinite is present in the face of the Other, Levinas writes the following:

> Certainly, the Other gives himself up to my powers, succumbs to my craftiness, to all of my violations. Or resists with all of his might and with the unpredictable resources of his own freedom. We can size each other up. But he can as well — in showing me his face — oppose himself to me beyond all measure in the total unveiling and total nudity of his defenseless eyes, in the straightforwardness of his glance. The solipsistic restlessness of consciousness always throughout all of its adventures finding itself captivated by the Self here terminates: true exteriority is in the look which prohibits me from embarking on any sort of conquest. Not just that the conquest challenges my already too weak potentials, but I simply cannot any more (je ne peux plus pouvoir): the structure of my liberty as we shall later see is totally reversed. A relation is established not with a great resistance, but with the absolutely Other, with the resistance of that which is without resistance, with ethical resistance. That is what leads to the dimension of the Infinite. That which arrests the irresistible impression of the Self and of the I. We call the face the epiphany of that which can present itself directly to an I and at the same time do so externally.[12]

Levinas sees the Idea of the Infinite as a radical experience emerges in social relations. In our relation to the Other we are addres, a being who is absolutely exterior to us and the infinity of this Other assures us of his exteriority. The exteriority of the Infinite is attested as an opposition to our powers which we experience at the appearance of the face of the Other. We do not experience the face as a mere form but as an absolute negation of our powers. "True exteriority lies in the look which prohibits appropriation and conquest not as a result of a lack of power, but because our powers are paralyzed before the appeal of the Other's defenselessness. We abandon the will to power, we will not to will. What resists us in non-resistance, an ethical resistance."[13]

Ethical resistance is the presence of the Infinite. The Other is not simply another freedom. On the ethical dimension, in order for me to become conscious of injustices inflicted upon him, his glance that comes towards me must come from the dimension of the ideal. The Other has to be closer to God than me. This, according to Levinas is not just an invention of philosophers but the first principle of moral consciousness, consciousness of the privileged position of the Other; justice begins with the Other. Experiencing the Other as being closer to God than we are ourselves, we experience him as being above us. His proximity to God confers upon him rights which we do not have with regard to our own conduct.

Levinas calls the presence of the Infinite 'desire.' Desire is the infinity of the Infinite which shows itself as an insatiable longing for the good of the Other. The desire for the Other does not express a lack, in the sense in which we feel an emptiness which can be filled, for it is experienced by a completely independent being who is already fulfilled. "It is the need of a being who has no needs."[14] Our relation with the Other does not necessarily make us happy; in fact it puts the Self into question, empties the Self of itself; it is a 'kenosis.' "It calls upon all of the resources of the self which we have no right to withhold from others. The desideratum does not fulfill an appetite but calls forth our generosity. It fulfills only in the sense in which it increases our hunger by adding new hungers."[15]

How does the Idea of the Infinite escape being gobbled up by the scheming of the Self? It is basically a question of freedom. It is as if it were that the presence of the face, the Idea of the Infinite in me would put my freedom into question. Freedom based on rationality still means that the Self is prominent. In Western philosophy the spontaneity of freedom usually remains unquestioned. Any limitation on freedom is seen to be tragic or scandalous. But entering into communication with the face of the Other has just this effect: it is a setback to my freedom.

The face of the Other is not the revelation of the free will of the Other but of the injustice he has suffered. Consciousness of my own injustice comes about not before the fact, but before the Other. The face of the Other reveals the injustice of the totality and fall of the phenomena which are derived from human freedom. We become ashamed of our own freedom before the Other for we realize that it is based upon injustice. The Other, by means of his face, does not appear to me as an obstacle or as a menace which I have to evaluate, but as he who 'sizes me up.' In order for me to experience myself, as unjust, to compare myself to the Infinite, and to be conscious of my own imperfection, I have to have the Idea of the Infinite, which is also the idea of perfection. The Infinite "stops me in my tracks," questioning the naïve rights of my power and my glorious spontaneity.

As Levinas goes on to explain, "this manner of measuring oneself with the perfection of the Infinite is not a theoretical consideration wherein freedom would once again spontaneously pick up on its rights. It is the sham which comes from freedom discovering itself both murderer and usurper."[16] Levinas refers to the Bible by showing that the story of creation comes before that of the ten commandments because, according to a second century exegete, the story of creation was very necessary in order for one to lead a just life. If the earth was not given to man, but simply taken by him he would have possessed it as a bandit. Spontaneous and naïve possession cannot justify itself by virtue of its own spontaneity. All this means that existence is not condemned to freedom (zur Freiheit verdammpt) but rather judged as freedom.

A life in freedom is a life of discovering oneself unjust. It is not a question of the structure of the free will spontaneously unfolding to grasp its happiness but rather an inversion wherein freedom beholds itself as unjust. As my demands increase so does the judgement which falls upon me, in other words, my responsibility; and the acuteness of these responsibilities increases the demands upon me. In such a movement my freedom does not have the last say in matters, I never rediscover my solitude, moral consciousness is essentially insatiable, or in other words, always desire.

> The insatiability of moral consciousness is not only the pain of delicate and scrupulous souls, but rather the contradiction, the hollow, the retreat within oneself, the systole itself of consciousness in brief; and the ethical consciousness is not called into this exposition as a variété, "highly recommendable" by consciousness, but rather as the concrete form which dons a movement which is more fundamental than freedom, the Idea of the Infinite, as the concrete form of that which precedes freedom and which neither conducts us to violence nor to the confusion of him who is separated, nor to necessity, nor to fatality.[17]

The face to face encounter with the Other, wherein freedom is put into question as an injustice, is experience in the strongest sense of the word. It is a contact with a reality which is not classifiable in any idea of the "a priori," which is not contained within any idea. That is why Levinas speaks about the Infinite. "No movement of freedom would know how to appropriate the face or give the impression of being able to constitute it."[18] The face is something which has been there from the beginning even before one has anticipated or constituted it. The face has been collaborating all the time, the face has been speaking. The face is pure experience, experience without concept.

Levinas emphasizes a deception before the Other, the incomprehensibility (désaisissement) which characterizes all of our attempts to grasp this reality. The insatiability of the moral consciousness, the deception before the Other coincides with desire. The desire of the Infinite is not the sweet sentimentality of love but a rigorous moral requirement. The rigour of the moral requirement is not brutally forced upon us, but comes about through attraction and the infinity of Being itself. "God only commands through men for whom we must act."[19]

The face of the Other is Levinas's point of departure in philosophy. This is his concept of moral consciousness — the display of my freedom to the judgement of the Other. "A lowering which has authorized us to catch a glimpse of the dimension of the loftiness and of the ideal in the glance of him to whom justice is due."[20]

Notes:
[1] Roland Paul Blum, "Emmanuel Levinas's Theory of Commitment," *Philosophy and Phenomenological Research* 44 (1983): 167.

[2] Edith Wyschogrod, *Emmanuel Levinas: The Problem of Ethical Metaphysics* (The Hague: Martinus Nijhoff, 1974), 91.

[3] Jean Lacroix, "L'infini et le prochain selon Emmanuel Lévinas," in *Panorame de la philosophie française contemporaine*, ed. Jean Lacroix (Paris: Presses universitaires de France, 1968), 120.

[4] DEHH 166.

[5] DEHH 167.

[6] DEHH 169.

[7] Wyschogrod, 14.

[8] DEHH 170.

[9] DEHH 170.

[10] DEHH 171.

[11] DEHH 173.

[12] DEHH 173.

[13] Wyschogrod, 92.

[14] DEHH 174.

[15] Wyschogrod, 93.

[16] DEHH 176.

[17] DEHH 177.

[18] DEHH 177.

[19] DEHH 177.

[20] DEHH 178.

4
The Face of the Other — the Trace of the Other

Levinas maintains that in Western philosophical tradition the other person loses his alterity. Western philosophy has been basically a philosophy of Being because of the widespread fear of the Other; comprehending Being means comprehending the fundamental structure of man as well. That is why this kind of philosophy becomes autonomous or 'atheistic' philosophy, a sort of irreligion. The God of the philosophers, from Aristotle to Leibniz, including that of the Scholastics, has been a God suited to reason, a comprehensible God who fits very well into the all-round plan and a God who could never upset the autonomy of consciousness which returns to itself, like Ulysses who, throughout his many pilgrimages, is always moving in the direction of his own birthplace.

In Western philosophical tradition not only does theoretical thinking always return upon itself, but so does all spontaneous movement of the consciousness as well. Not only does the world itself cease to be something other, because consciousness can find itself even there, but all attitudes of consciousness as well, such as values, feelings, actions, work, etc., are in the final analysis consciousness of oneself, that is to say, identity and autonomy. This aversion to the Other reaches its pinnacle in Hegel.

Therefore Levinas wants to move towards the Other, but in such a way that this movement towards the Other would not end up in a return to identity, would not end up at its point of departure. It would be a movement of the Self towards the Other which would never return to the Self.[1] Instead of the Odyssey of Homer, in which Ulysses starts out in Ithaca and ends up in Ithaca, Levinas proposes the story of Abraham who leaves his native land forever and travels towards a land yet unknown. This movement from the Self to the Other is what Levinas calls 'l'oeuvre' — the task.

When the task is thought out to its limits it entails a radical generosity on behalf of the Self, who moves towards the Other. An ungratefulness on behalf of the Other should make no difference. The task is not a collecting of merits but rather absolute goodness. It cannot expect any rewards in this departure without return, no matter how evident its triumph. If the goal were reward, then the one-way movement would very quickly turn into reciprocity. If there were a question of rewards, remuneration, then the task would be lost in a calculation of losses and gains. One-way action can only come about in patience driven to its extreme which means none other than acting without entering "the promised land." It is acting and living "for free," without charging for my services and not even expecting a tip. It is to do things for others for nothing (umsonst leben), even to the point where in addition to my services it is I who suffer the losses.

Levinas explains that the task in all future handlings must mean a being indifferent to my own death. I must act towards a point beyond my own death, forgetting about any personal immortalization. I must renounce being a contemporary to my triumphs by envisioning a time without me, by envisioning a world without me, by envisioning a time beyond the horizon of my own time. It is an eschatology without any hopes, a promised but unknown land, liberation from my own time.

To exist for a time without me, to exist for a time after my time, for a future beyond the famous "being-towards-death," rather a "being-towards-after-my-death" is the passage from time to the Other.

Levinas foreshadows here his theory of responsibility, which he will extensively develop in his book *Otherwise than Being or Beyond Essence*. He is referring to a responsibility which I have for the processes in which I find myself which goes beyond what I willed or what I can steer. Alphonso Lingis, Levinas's English translator best sums it up this way:

> Responsibility cannot be limited to the measure of what I was able to foresee and will.... I am responsible for processes that go beyond the limits of my foresight and intention, that carry on even when I am no longer adding my sustaining force to them — and even when I am no longer there. Serious responsibility recognizes itself to be responsible for the course of things beyond one's own death. My death will mark the limit of my force without limiting my responsibility.[2]

In order to describe the task of the movement of the Self to the Other without a return to the Self, Levinas chooses a Greek word which signifies not only the exercise of a certain office for absolutely nothing, for free (gratuit), but even requiring a "cash outlay" on the part of him who is invested with that office. He chooses the word 'liturgy.' He contends that all religious connotation should, for the moment, be put aside in the examination of this term even if near the end of the analysis a few traces of the idea of God should eventually creep in. Liturgy is not a cult apart from ethics. It is ethics itself.

A) "Need and Desire"

The liturgical orientation of the task is not a need. Need is something which is oriented towards me, a returning to myself, a nostalgia. "It is an assimilation of the world in view of a meeting up with itself or with happiness."[3]

Desire in the sense in which Levinas wants to use the word is totally opposed to any stoical meaning of the word wherein the subject is defined in terms of being for himself and for whom happiness is something directed towards himself. Desire is desire for the Other which comes forth from a being who is already fulfilled and independent, who no longer desires for himself. "The need of him who no longer has any needs manifests itself in the needs of another who is the Other and who is neither my enemy (as in Hobbes or Hegel) nor my complement, as in Plato's "Republic," wherein something is lacking in the subsistence of every individual."[4] The desire for the Other is something that comes forth from a being who is not lacking anything; it has its source beyond all measure of lacking or satisfaction.

Desire for the Other which is at the basis of our sociality is not just a simple relationship with a being in which the Other converts into the Self. Rather, my relationship with the Other fills me with doubts, it leaves me empty and never ceases to empty me although at the same time it always allows me to discover new resources within myself. "I never knew myself to be so rich but neither do I any longer have the right to maintain anything. The 'desired' does not fulfill my desire but rather hollows it out, at the same time in a strange manner nourishing me ever again with new hungers."[5] The desire is goodness. Levinas brings in an example of this kind of desire in referring to a scene from Dostoyevsky's "Crime and Punishment": Sonia Marmeladova sees Raskolnikov in his desperation and Dostoyevsky speaks of an "insatiable compassion" which she has for Raskolnikov. He does not say an "inexhaustible compassion" but rather, again, insatiable, as if this compassion which Sonia has for Raskolnikov were a hunger nourished alone by the presence of Raskolnikov, beyond all saturation, causing this hunger to grow beyond all limit, driving it to infinity.

In order to attain more insight into the analysis of desire and in order to be able to distinguish it more accurately from need, an examination of the Other towards whom the desire is directed is called for.

First of all, the Other manifests himself in conformity with the manner in which all meaning manifests itself. The Other is present in a cultural ensemble, a cultural totality, and manifests himself in this totality according to his context. The Other is enlightened by the "light of the world," so to speak. Therefore the comprehension of the Other requires a hermeneutics, an exegesis. The Other reveals himself in a cultural context and is analyzed in terms of cultural initiatives, by corporal, linguistic or artistic gestures.

On the other hand, the epiphany of the Other merits an independence from all meaning which we have already received from the world. The Other approaches us not just out of his context alone in the totality of existence, but rather immediately, defining himself. His cultural context, his inner world of mundane significance, if one desires to remain purely within the horizon of an historical world explored in accordance with the investigated phenomenological horizons of this same world, are with his apparition disturbed and jostled about. The Other differs from other phenomena in that he is able to announce himself. Levinas describes the phenomenon of the apparition of the Other using the French word "visage" or 'face' (which can also be rendered into English using the somewhat archaic and literary word 'visage'), and says that the epiphany of the visage is a visitation (itself a word normally used only in a religious context in both French and English, referring to the Blessed Virgin's visit to Saint Elisabeth who was waiting to give birth to John the Baptist). Whereas a phenomenon enters mundane immanence as a fixed image, modelled and mute, the face is something living. The face, although like other existents "fixed into position," always attempts to undo any sort of concealment or stagnant thematical categorization. The face exposes itself and proceeds to reveal of itself in a measure greatly exceeding its proper form in that of being "just another face." The face speaks, and in its speaking it goes beyond its appearance, beyond its form into what Levinas calls 'an opening in the opening.' That is to say, the origin of the face lies beyond Being, beyond the very possibility of appearing within the limits of a horizon. The face is abstract. The face cannot be placed against a horizon within the world.

B) "The Diaconate"

The visitation of the Visage or face is not the disclosure of a world. In the concrete world the face is abstract or naked. It is stripped of its own image, deprived of all cultural ornamentation. It enters the world from a totally foreign sphere, "that is to say precisely, from an absolute which is somewhere else, from basic foreignness itself."[6] The face in its abstraction is literally something extraordinary. It is non-convertible, non-transformable into either symbolism or suggestion. It is not a simple representation. It is an outcry in which consciousness is overturned and finds itself having to respond. Stripped of its own form the face is paralyzed in its own nakedness (transi dans sa nudité); a misery. The nakedness of the face is deprivation and already a supplication in the directness with which it confronts me. But this supplication is also a demand upon me and it is here that the ethical dimension of the visitation becomes evident. While the Self is caught up in speculations about its own free thought in light of truth and existence, the Face imposes upon me in such a way that I cannot remain deaf to its calling, nor can I forget it. The fact of facing the Other "…is not turning a surface, but appealing contesting, it is the move by which alterity breaks into the sphere of phenomena."[7] I cannot but be held responsible for the misery of the Other's face. Consciousness is no longer primary when the presence of the face becomes a command. The availability of mobility of consciousness is suspended. Consciousness is put into question to the extent of not even being able to return to itself and take conscious note of this being put into question. The face, the absolutely Other does not reflect itself in the immobilized consciousness. The visitation shatters the egoism of the I and upheaves the intentionality aimed towards it.

The I loses its sovereignty, its self-identity, wherein consciousness triumphantly returns to itself to rest with itself. Before the command of the Other, the I is shaken out of its slumber. However, the putting into question of consciousness is not an alienation. It is rather the welcoming reception of the absolutely Other. The Other's calling upon me in his nakedness and deprivation summons me to reply. But the I does not become conscious of the necessity to reply as if it were only a duty or an obligation which he is free to decide upon. The I becomes conscious of his responsibility, or his diaconate, as in the fifty-third chapter of Isaiah.[8]

Such an orientation of the 'I' as presented above seeks to identify the 'I' with morality. The 'I' before the Other is infinitely responsible. To desire is to burn with another kind of flame than the flame of need, which can be extinguished by saturation. It is in the relationship between the desirous I and the Other that we arrive at the Idea of the Infinite.

As seen in the last chapter, the Idea of the Infinite is desire and consists in thinking more than the thought, entering into relation with the indiscernible while at the same time guaranteeing His status as indiscernible. The Infinite is not the correlate of the Idea of the Infinite, as if the idea were an intentionality that is carried out in its object. The wonder of the Infinite in the finite is an upheaval of intentionality, an upheaval of this thirst for light. The Infinite sheds its idea (l'infini désarçonne son idée).

C) "The Trace"

In one of the supplements to *En découvrant l'existence avec Husserl et Heidegger*, Levinas goes into an extensive description of what he calls "the Trace." These descriptions are often vague, hard to follow, and are among the most difficult of his philosophical reflections. His use of the concepts face and trace make them very difficult to distinguish from one another. This will become apparent as an endeavor is made to discuss at greater length just what the trace is.

The trace is fundamentally the trace of the Absolute; it is neither the Absolute itself nor the face itself. On the other hand, the face is in a certain sense the trace itself. Stephan Strasser, in his book on Levinas "Jenseits von Sein und Zeit" explains:

> The face is simply a trace of a "handing over" (Überantwortung) without eliminating the ambiguity which fascinates me. It hinders the Other from becoming a neomatic correlate of my own intentional efforts. It brings about that the other commands me even before he appears to me as a phenomena.[9]

Levinas says that the face is abstract, in the sense of abstracted from, isolated. But it is not an abstraction in the sensory manner of the empiricists.

It is not an incision into time at the point where time would perpendicularly cross eternity: it is an incision into time which does not bleed (c'est une coupure du temps qui ne saigne pas)[10] The abstraction of the face is visitation and arrival. It disturbs immanence without letting itself be set within the horizons of the world. Its abstraction is not part of a logical process departing from the substances of beings going from the particular to the general. On the contrary, the face goes towards these beings without compromising itself with them, withdraws from them and absolves, pardons, dismisses itself. The wonder of the face lies precisely in the "somewhere else" from whence it comes and just as quickly thither takes refuge. But this fact of having come from somewhere else is not just a symbolic referral to this somewhere else as if it were a simple term, but rather an indication of the fundament of a phenomenon in hiding at the same time betraying something of itself. The face does not signify, it indicates. If it were not so then the face would be nothing more than a mask. If to signify were the same thing as to indicate, the face would be insignificant. Sartre has called the Other a pure hole in the world (pur trou). The face is like a pure hole in the world not because one's own world drains away through the Other but because the Other stands in a relationship to the absolutely Other.[11] The Other proceeds from the absolutely Absent. But his relationship with the Absent does not reveal the Absent and that is why the Absent has meaning in the face. The face is not a place of revelation through the physiognomy of which the transcendent can be seen. This would mean a thematization of the Absent which is precisely what Levinas wants to avoid. The Absent is beyond all revelation and dissimilation and does not enter into the immanent order of things.

The face, claims Levinas, is something that is left in the trace of the Absent, the totally Other having once long ago left his mark; the face is the trace of the Infinite which does not enter into our immanent order of things: "Le visage est dans la trace de l'Absent absolument revolu, absolument passé, retiré dans ce que Paul Valery appelle 'profond jadis, jadis, jamais assez.'"[12] The face is in the trace of the Absent with its indefinability and incontainability; it is precisely the "Unfixierbarkeit" of the face which points to a beyond. As Levinas explains:

> The face is meaning and meaning without context. I want to say that the Other in the rectitude of his face is not a personage: Professor at the

> Sorbonne, vice-president of the Council of State, son of Mr. and Mrs. so and so, everything that is in the passport, the way one dresses, presents oneself. And all meaning in the normal usage of the word, is relative to a context. The meaning of something is in its relationship to something else. Here however, on the contrary, the face is meaning to itself. You are you. In this sense one can say that the face is not seen. The face is that which cannot become a content which your thoughts could embrace; it is incontainable, it takes you beyond.[13]

From the above we can conclude that the face takes us "beyond being." That which is beyond being is a third person who does not define himself by his own self, by his *ipseity*. This third person is the "possibility of the radical irrectitude that escapes the bipolar game of immanence and transcendence proper to being where immanence wins over transcendence."[14] The third person is the "ille," "illeity." the movement of infinition which Levinas will name God. The "au-dela" from which the face comes is the third person; the pronoun 'ille,' exactly expresses the inexpressible irreversibility — that is to say, already having escaped all revelation and all dissimulation, it is in this sense, absolutely unfathomable, absolute transcendence in an absolute past. The illeity of the third person is the condition of the irreversibility.[15] In other words, one could say that the beyond of being opened up by the face is a personal order irreducible to rational discourse or to the world of need. It is a third person, he who cannot be defined. "The profile that the irreversible past takes on through the trace is the profile of the 'He.' The third person is the beyond. He is absolutely unavailable, withdrawn into an irreversible past. This irreversibility is designated by Levinas as his illeity."[16]

The third person is not smaller than being but enormity, measureless, — i.e., the Infinite, the absolutely Other escaping all ontology; "the supreme presence of the face is inseparable from this supreme and irreversible absence which is even at the basis of the eminence of the visitation."[17]

D) "The Trace and Illeity"

Levinas says that the significance of the trace is that it gives meaning without permitting appearance. It is important to understand that in this sense, the trace does not belong to phenomenology. Any relationship to illeity is an ethical one, as with the face. The face should not be understood as a sort of phenomenological divine reflector. In discussion with Philippe Nemo in *Ethique et Infini* Levinas is asked about the phenomenology of the face; "What does the phenomenology of the face consist of, that is to say, this analysis that takes place when I look at the Other face to face?" His reply is:

> I don't know if one can speak of a phenomenology of the face because phenomenology describes that which appears. Furthermore I ask myself if one can speak of a "look" directed towards the face, because a look means perception. I think that an access to the face is above all else ethical. When you see a nose, eyes, a forehead, a chin and are able to describe them, then you're turning towards the other as if towards an object. The best way of meeting the other is to not even remember the colour of his eyes! When you observe the colour of the eyes you're not in a social relationship with the other. The relationship with the face may be dominated by perception, but that which is specifically the face is irreducible.[18]

The trace is not a sign, although it can have the role of a sign or be taken to be a sign. In the world, all signs are tied into a specific order where everything reveals something else, much like the detective who examines as a sign anything that could tell something about the criminal, about his actions, voluntary or involuntary; or like the hunter who follows in the footsteps of his prey, etc. The big difference is that when the trace is taken for a sign in comparison to other signs, it has something of the exceptional about it. That which it signifies is apart from all intention to be signified and apart from all projections aimed towards it. The Other does not reveal his origin as the sign reveals what is signified; that which is Absent is not unveiled as Being through the appearance of the face, for the absent is beyond both being and revelation: "It is a mistake to assume that the elsewhere which is evoked by the face can yield a meaning for investigation; to assume that is to assume that the elsewhere is world. It is also to ignore the fundamental lesson of phenomenology; there is no world behind the world which appears."[19]

Levinas elaborates upon this idea with a few very vivid analogies:

> When in financial transactions one pays by cheque in order to leave a trace of payment, this trace is registered within the order of the world. However the authentic trace upsets the order of the world. It comes in

a "surimpression." Its original significance imaged in the imprint which is left behind is like that of him who wants to erase all his traces in order to commit the perfect crime. He who leaves traces by erasing his traces does not want to communicate anything by the traces he leaves behind. He upsets the order in an irreparable way. He has absolutely faded himself out (Il a absolument passé). Being, in so far as leaving a trace, means to move on (passer), depart, to absolve oneself.[20]

The trace, over and above that which the sign signifies, is the passage of him who gave the sign. The significance of the trace doubles the significance of the sign as a means of communication. The sign holds itself in this trace. Signification could for example, be found in a letter which is appreciated according to graphics or style and not go beyond that. However a graphologist or a psychiatrist could go beyond this and do an analysis, in order to discover the intention of the trace, in order to discover more about the intentions of him who left the message. But that which remains specifically trace, apart from the graphics or style of the letter, does not reveal precisely anything. In the trace, a past which is absolutely past has passed. In the trace its irreversible revolution embeds itself. The revelation (dévoilement) which restores the world and returns to the world and which is proper to a sign or a meaning, abolishes itself in the trace.

The trace is the heaviness of Being apart from acts and language — heavy not by its presence but by its irreversibility, by its ab-solution (Selbstloslösung). It is Being's indelibility itself, an immense incapability to contain itself too great for interiority, for a Self. The trace in effect is that which indicates towards the Infinite, towards the absolutely Other. It is the Transcendent, Divinity. But once again the trace is deducible neither from Being nor from existants. The trace is not revealed or signalled or indicated directly, but disturbs, upsets the order of things. It does not coincide with anything. As Levinas explains:

> The trace is an insertion in space of time, the point wherein the world heels towards a past and a time. This time is the retreat of the Other and consequently in no way a degradation of the time period wholly within remembrance; superiority does not exist in a presence in the world but in an irreversible transcendence. The trace is not a modulation of the Being of the existent. In as much as he (the Other) is a third person, the trace is in a certain sense beyond distinctions of Being and existents.

> Only a being which transcends the world can leave a trace. The trace is the presence of him who was never here, of him who is always past.[21]

When Levinas speaks of the trace as an insertion in space of time as a point where the world turns towards the past, it is difficult to understand precisely what Levinas means by the spatiality of the trace, since he has been careful to insist that the trace cannot be brought to light, cannot be unveiled, be brought into the order of the world, understood as phenomenon: "It is of course possible that Levinas speaks of the other person, of the face which appears in space but is beyond all appearing, that is 'means' beyond what can be the object of cognitive intentionality."[22]

Only transcendence preserves the specific meaning of the trace above and beyond its significancy. This transcendence in the trace is what Levinas calls illeity, as mentioned, this movement of infinition which Levinas names God, a God who does not leave traces. A stone strikes another. The trace left upon the stone could be understood as a trace. In reality, without the man who held the stone, the scratch is no more than an effect. Cause and effect, although temporally separated, still belong to the same world. Everything in things is exposed, even their unknown. The traces which indicate these things are part of this plentitude of presence, their history is without a past. "The trace as trace however does not direct us only towards a past, but is the passage towards a past further away than all past and all future, which are still in my time, towards the past of the Other, where eternity is drafted (ou se dessine l'éternité) — an absolute past that reunites all time."[23]

The transcendence of the trace is not present in the world. It is, according to Levinas, the presence of what in effect has never been there, for in order to have been there the transcendent would have had to belong to the order of Being. The transcendent is that which is perpetually past.

The absoluteness of the presence of the Other is not simply the presence where in the final analysis things themselves are present. Their presence belongs to the present of my life. Everything that constitutes my life with its past and its future is gathered together in the present in which all things come to me. But it is in the trace of the Other that the face gleams. That which presents itself there is in the process of absolving my life and visits me as already absolute. The face is itself visitation and transcendence. But at the same time the face can be in-itself because it is in the trace of the Other that the face gleams. That which presents itself there is in the process of absolving my life and visits me as already absolute. The face is itself visitation and transcendence. But at the same time the face can be in-itself because it is in the trace of illeity. Illeity is the origin of the alterity of Being. In the same way, the face belongs to the world of immanence as a thing in the world, while it retains its alterity and its origin beyond appearance. The beyond from which the face comes, appears as a "trace." The face is an absolutely completed past, a heretofore which is completely irrecoverable. The meaning of the trace issues from an immemorial past, a past impervious to memory. The past is also eternity.

What comes to mind at once as a result of Levinas's discussion of the trace is the classical conception of the "imago Dei." This indeed is Levinas's point of view: the face is in the image of God. But what does it mean to be in the image of God? It is not to be an "icon" of God but to find oneself in his trace. The God of the Judeo-Christian tradition retains "all the infinity of his absence."

> The God who has passed by is not a model whose image is the face. To be in the image of God does not mean to be an icon of God, but rather to find oneself in His trace. The God who reveals himself in our Judeo-Christian spirituality conserves infinity in his absence... He only shows Himself by His trace, as in the thirty-third chapter of Exodus. To move towards Him is not to follow the trace which is not a sign, but to move towards others who are in His trace.[24]

What Levinas is attempting to illustrate is that God is only approachable there, where His manifestation of revelation is disturbed by alterity, in the one who addresses me. Levinas gives us the first person, the ego, coming into relation with the second person who eludes apprehension precisely in function of the third personality designated in him — the ille. "The Other inasmuch as he lends himself to thematization and becomes a phenomenon said, becomes something present and represented — but that by which he is Other is precisely the ille that eludes my presence, not as a telos or an end already anticipated and representable, apprehensible in advance, but rather as an irrecuperable past."[25]

Summing up, one could say that the concept of the trace serves as the corner-stone of Levinas's religious and, consequently, philosophical thinking. In terms of biblical imagery it is the humility of God. The concept of the trace does not allow the relationship between the Creator and creation to be thought of in terms of correlation in the light of experience which has always "shackled" the Transcendent, enchained the Transcendent to significations in 'terms of this world.' The Transcendent cannot be synchronized with the usual significations and discussions which hold it captive. Still, through the experience of the Other, which is experience "par excellence," the Transcendent is experienced.

"A great experience that is never experienced"[26] — perhaps this is the best way to describe the trace in one sentence. Moses' encounters, with the burning bush to which he does not raise his eyes and with the God who is "revealed" to him as having already passed by, describe how the Other can remain equivocal and incognito, invading the Self without contesting it on its own terms.

E) Presence and Absence

Levinas's definition of God as a Trace or as the Absent is not as cryptic as it first appears. In phenomenology, the naming of something is understood as an interplay of presence and absence. The origin of this understanding is Husserl's notion of empty and filled intentions. In the naming of an object or a situation, there is a host of qualities which are either rendered present or left absent. The use of words involves various levels of transcendence. We may render an object present by describing it although the object itself is not physically before us; it is absent. Robert Sokolowski in his book *Presence and Absence* writes: "My uncle is out selling the house. By enumerating enough features and by relating an object to things or persons we are acquainted with, we can identify objects we have never actually experienced but which have been repeated to us."[27] Or, should the object be physically before us, we may no longer need to describe it, and the qualities we gave it in our initial description will be absent and may forever remain unnoticed.

Another example: A professor asked his students to draw the kind of number six that was on their watches without first looking at them. One student drew a large round number six, since all the digits on his watch were large and round. When he looked at his watch he noticed that there was no number six at all — in place of the six there was a small second hand. The absence of the number six had for years remained — at least consciously — unnoticed, though the watch was glanced at dozens of times each day; for the student the watch had been a timepiece, and not an object for aesthetic contemplation. If the watch were to be lost and needed description, the second hand would be a useful distinguishing feature. Description would render the watch present, though being lost it would remain physically absent.

The above examples, of "my uncle's house" or the watch, are very simple. As one climbs the philosophical ladder and begins to analyze human speech and situations, the interplay of presence and absence becomes more complex. There comes the apparition of the Other, and I am obliged to listen. Robert Sokolowski writes:

> Once we begin to take certain facts as discovered or reported by others we also begin to identify the speakers who are responsible for them. The other person has already been identified as a spatio-temporal physical living object and as an agent who has done certain things; he has already been addressed as an audience for my speaking; but now he becomes identifiable on a higher level as someone who can also speak to me with a certain authority about things and their arrangements. He becomes capable of naming things and exercising syntax, the articulator of certain facts which might not have been realized had he not perceived thought and spoken. He becomes quotable, a participant in conversation. New forms of names and syntax are now needed to speak of him and others as seeing, thinking, knowing, saying and the like.[28]

Through linguistic analyses we attempt to interpret and understand correctly the subtleties and nuances of the Other, whence he slips in, and whither he just as quickly slips away — the fine line between his presence and absence.

Climbing even higher, we begin to speculate about manifestations of Being or the existence of God — the point where presence and absence become almost impossible to identify and distinguish. A philosopher might conceivably describe presence by reference to structures such as sameness and otherness, rest and motion, identity and difference, permanence and change. Yet these structures, though useful, do not make everything clear.

Absence in philosophy is even more difficult: in naming material things we have the alternative of spatial absence, in naming temporal things, temporal absence, but in philosophy we have neither. Absence, an anonymous awareness at most, is unthematic in philosophy, concerned as it is with the presencing of things. Yet however vague, absence cannot be ignored: it is the other side of presence — the two are always in interplay. Sokolowski writes:

> Besides the transitions from simple presence to absence and vice versa there is a special kind of emergence of something present not out of sheer absence but out of obscurity and confusion and vagueness which is a peculiar kind of interference with presence. There is an appropriate obscurity for every kind of presence just as there is an absence appropriate to it; the obscure and the transition from the obscure to the clear and vice versa must also be explored.[29]

The obscure domain of absence is where Levinas feels at home. Just as it is precisely the Self's inability to constitute or grasp the Other which makes the Other a source of interest for the Self, just as the content itself of the Idea of the Infinite contains more than does the idea, so absence is a surplus which remains after the positive attributes of ontological presence and the superlatives of wisdom and power have been done away with — a surplus wherein God is found. Absence is the vague and obscure background on which the Absent has left his traces. Sokolowski describes this kind of absence as an urgent need:

> I may urgently need an object or urgently feel the need for an object. "Water," I utter the word. The sound is pulled out by association but the association arises from a felt need, not from a sensed presence. The sound sounds out by association with what I have experienced in the past, the thirst I now feel, although the object is absent and is felt as absent.[30]

I do not sense God's presence, but His absence — a felt need. I call His name, to which this need gives rise. The name comes to me by association with the absence I have experienced in the past — the very absence in which He has left His Trace.

Notes:
[1] DEHH 191.
[2] Alphonso Lingis, "Translator's Introduction," in OBBE.
[3] DEHH 192.

[4] DEHH 193.

[5] DEHH 193.

[6] DEHH 194.

[7] Lingis, xviii.

[8] Surely he has borne our griefs
and carried our sorrows
yet we esteemed him stricken,
smitten by God and afflicted.
But he was wounded for our transgressions,
he was bruised for our iniquities;
upon him was the chastisement that made us whole
and with his stripes we are healed.
All we like sheep have gone astray;
we have turned everyone to his own way;
and the Lord has laid on him
the iniquity of us all.
He was oppressed, and he was afflicted;
yet he opened not his mouth;
like a lamb that is led to slaughter,
and like sheep that before its shearers is dumb,
so he opened not his mouth. (Isaiah 53: 4-7)

[9] Stefan Strasser, *Jenseits von Sein und Zeit* (The Hague: Martinus Nijhoff, 1978), 146.

[10] DEHH 197.

[11] Edith Wyschogrod, *Emmanuel Levinas: The Problem of Ethical Metaphysics* (The Hague: Martinus Nijhoff, 1974), 146.

[12] "The face is in the Trace of the Absent, absolutely completed (in time), absolutely passed by, withdrawn into what Paul Valery calls profoundly of old, of long ago, never long ago enough." DEHH 198.

[13] EI 91.

[14] DEHH 199.

[15] DEHH 199.

[14] Wyschogrod, 147.

[17] DEHH 199.

[18] EI 90.

[19] Wyschogrod, 146.

[20] DEHH 200.

[21] DEHH 201.

[22] Wyschogrod, 149.

[23] DEHH 201.

[24] DEHH 202. The reference is to Exodus (33:17-23):
And the Lord said to Moses "This very thing that you have spoken I will do; for you have found favour in my sight, and I know you by name." Moses said, "I pray thee, show me thy glory." And he said, "I will make all my goodness pass before you, and I will proclaim before you my name 'The Lord'; and I will be gracious to whom I will be gracious, and will show mercy on whom I will show mercy." "But" he said, "you cannot see my face; for man shall not see me and live." And the Lord said, "Behold there is a place by me where you shall stand upon the rock; and while my glory passes by I will put you in a cleft of the rock, and I will cover you with my hand until I have passed by; then I will take away my hand and you shall see my back; but my face shall not be seen."

[25] Lingis, xxxiv.

[26] Steven G. Smith, *The Argument to the Other: Reason Beyond Reason in the Thought of Karl Barth and Emmanuel Levinas* (Chico, California: Scholars Press, 1983), 169.

[27] Robert Sokolowski, *Presence and Absence* (Bloomington, Indiana: Indiana University Press, 1978), 39.

[28] Ibid., 57.

[29] Ibid., see Chapter 15, "Thinking Beyond Philosophy."

[30] Ibid., 152.

5
Responsibility and Substitution of the One-for-the-Other and the Horizon of the Infinite

In *Totality and Infinity* the principle structure of sociality is the separation between persons which is based on the 'original atheism' of the self's inner life of enjoyment, and the transcendence of the Other. In *Otherwise than Being or Beyond Essence*, the main theme is a relation to the Other of infinite proximity and obsession, rather than of separation and prophetic 'possession' by the Good and moral inspiration rather than atheism.

In *Otherwise than Being or Beyond Essence*, responsibility is set forth as the determinative structure of subjectivity. In both Husserl and Heidegger responsibility appears as something quite extraordinary. For Husserl absolute self-responsibility, not the satisfaction of human wants is the goal of theoretical culture, and should be the basis of Western spirituality. It involves a total suspension of the natural attitude, and a leap into an utterly unnatural form of life, one devoted to the idea of infinity. In Heidegger it requires an antecedent leap beyond what is as a whole, into the abysses of death.[1] For Levinas it is equally bizarre because it is inexplicable in mundane, ontic or transcendental terms: "The subjectivity structured as responsibility which Levinas means to bring out, although it will indeed make the theoretical attitude of the ontological articulation possible, has an antecedent and autonomous structure. For before being the structure by which truth is realized, it is a relationship with the Good, which is over and beyond Being."[2]

Furthermore, responsibility is a fact, a bond with an imperative order, in other words, a command. All subjective moments are under an order; subjectivity is subjection. Once again Levinas develops the theme of the Other, for we are made aware of the imperative by the Other who faces us.

The act of facing is not the mere turning of a surface, but an appealing and a contesting. Responsibility, therefore, is the response to the imperative issued in the concrete act of facing. Responsibility is a relationship with the Other in his very alterity.

Responsibility is both a form of recognition and an act. It is an acknowledgement of the claim which the Other has upon me and it is an expressive act by which I expose myself, expressing my own Being to the Other. It is incarnation by which I give my very substance to another. Responsibility is enacted not only in offering my property or possessions to the Other, but in giving my very substance to him. The figure of maternity as presented in *Totality and Infinity* is an authentic figure of responsibility.

The extent of responsibility is infinite. Responsibilities increase in the measure in which they are taken up. They lead to a constantly opening horizon, an infinition.

Responsibility having the status of an act means that it did not originate in an act of subjectivity – in the act of taking or assuming something upon oneself. It does not originate through an act of presentation or representation. It is in this sense "pre-original," prior to all initiatives and their principles, anarchic; "responsibility appears as a plot without a beginning – anarchic."[3] The responsibility for the Other, which flows forth from the face's appeal, essentially begins as absolute heteronomy. I am no longer the law, rather, the Other is; I am no longer the measure of all things, but rather, the one being measured. The responsibility for the Other has its origin not in my initiative, rather it precedes my freedom. Without being asked, I become responsible, because of the Other's appearance:

> This responsibility is attributed to me before I am in a condition to make a decision. It has no source in any natural predisposition or any altruistic tendency, any subjective feeling of sympathy or compassion or any spontaneous preparedness for sacrifice, all of which find their origin and principle in awareness. If this were the case, we would then, with the category of responsibility, be projected directly into an elitist morality, since this would become the privilege of those who, by nature or by a "divine instinct," are fortuitously more greatly endowed with a "tendency" toward this responsibility. Contrary to this, Levinas posits that this responsibility precedes both altruism and egoism and by extention, freedom, as the origin of both – which implies that responsibility concerns the condition or structure of the subject itself.[4]

This means that I am not only responsible for acts of my own will but also for the situation in which I find myself. It means being responsible for a situation which was already there before I came; "Responsibility is a bond between my present and what came to pass before it. In it is effected a passive synthesis of time that precedes the time put together by retentions and protentions."[5]

I am responsible for processes in which I find myself even though their momentum can go beyond that which I willed or had foreseen: "Responsibility cannot be limited to the measure of what I was able to foresee and will. In fact real action in the world is always action in which the devil has his part, in which the force of initiative has force only inasmuch as it espouses things that have a force of their own."[6] I am responsible for things that go on even when I am no longer adding my sustaining force to them, even when I am no longer there. Real responsibility recognizes itself to be responsible for things beyond one's own death.

In this responsibility there is an infinity that opens up, not as a result of the immensity of my responsibilities but rather as a result of a process in which the limits of my responsibility do not cease to extend if it is an infinition of infinity. The bond with the alterity of the Other is in this infinity and is also what makes me conscious of it. Once again, Alphonso Lingis sums it up very beautifully:

> I am answerable before the Other in his alterity – responsible before all the others for all the others. To be responsible before the Other is to make of my subsistence the support of his order and his needs. His alterity commands and solicits, his approach contests and appeals; I am responsible before the Other, for the Other. I am responsible before the Other in his alterity, that is, not answerable – for his empirical and mundane being only, but for the alterity of his initiatives, for the imperative appeal with which he addresses me. I am responsible for the responsible moves of another, for the very impact and trouble with which he approaches me. To be responsible before another is to answer to the appeal by which he approaches. It is to put oneself in his place, not to observe oneself from without, but to bear the burden of his existence and supply for its wants. I am responsible for the very faults of another for his deeds and misdeeds. The condition of being hostage is an authentic figure of responsibility.[7]

A) "The Experience of Alterity"

The relationship with the Other in his alterity consists in being appealed to and contested by the Other. This movement comes from without, alterity is not posited as an act of my subjectivity. Nor is the moral imperative which emanates from the Other a result of some sort of synthesis affected by my subjectivity according to its own a priori principles. The approach of the Other is an initiative I undergo and I am passive with regard to it. Alterity comes to me from without and exceeds all my capacities. Like the idea of infinity in Descartes which is put into me, I could not have accounted for alterity myself, and whose very reality as infinity exceeds any capacity. In this contact I am totally consumed, emptied. It is my kenosis:

> The I approached in responsibility is the for-the-other, is a denuding, an exposure to being affected, a pure susceptiveness. It does not posit itself, possessing itself and recognizing itself, it is consumed and delivered over, dislocates itself, loses its place, is exiled, relegates itself into itself, but as though its very skin were still a way to shelter itself in being, exposed to wounds and outrage emptying itself in a no-grounds (non lieu), to the point of substituting itself for the other, holding on to itself only as it were in the trace of its exile. What verbs like "to deliver itself," "consume itself," "exile itself" (se livrer, se consume, s'exiler), suggest by their prenominal form is not an act of reflection on oneself, of concern for oneself, it is not an act at all, but a modality of passivity which in substitution is beyond even passivity. To be oneself as in the trace of one's exile is to be as a pure withdrawal from oneself, and as such, an inwardness. Inwardness is not at all like a way of disposing of private matters. This inwardness without secrets is a pure witness to the inordinateness which already commands me, to give to the other taking the bread out of my own mouth, and making a gift of my own skin.[8]

The initiative to which alterity is given is neither apprehensive nor comprehensive – but rather it is sensibility. One is passive towards the approach of the Other, one sustains the impact of alterity without being able to assimilate it. One is susceptible to being affecting, being exalted or being pained:

> These terms locate the impact with alterity in the sensibility, but in a sensibility that is no longer being conceived as the receptive side of a synthetic and double event, where receptivity is receptive only in already being comprehensively grasped, where the receptive entity

continually regains possession of itself by synoptically apprehending what affects it. Such is sensibility defined as an element of a cognitive act, an act of consciousness. The sensibility affected by alterity is not that sensibility, where identification is already at work. Precisely, alterity is unidentifiable. Its sense is the unilateral direction of an approach, caught in a being ordered, an obedience.[9]

For Levinas, the Other and the ethical bond with alterity are over and beyond Being and its truth. It has its sources in the Platonic concepts of the One and the Good, in the opposition between totality and infinity, and in the religious word God. Being and its truth are not all encompassing and not even intelligible in themselves. Therefore, the concept of infinity does not originate, in the Husserlian sense, in a formalization and idealization of the spatial sense of horizontal openness, nor in the absolutization of the idea of truth, but in the "inapprehendability of alterity and the unsatisfiability of the moral exigency."[10] It is a certain "divinization" of the relationship with alterity. Levinas wants to find the proper meaning of God and does so in the ethical bond. The sense of responsibility which I have for the Other bears witness to the Infinite who is God.

The development of Levinas's argument in *Otherwise than Being*, rests on two dimensions of the ethical structure: on the one hand obligation always remains more than what one has accomplished. This gives the moral bond a sense of the unfinished, a sense of infinition. Whereas Being likes to present, re-present, synchronize, integrate, totalize, the approach of the Other in his alterity comes as a disturbance, transcendence and infinition. On the other hand the Other is irreducible. He is not interchangeable with me, even if my whole subjective reality consists in substituting myself for him. In this sense the Other, by virtue of his alterity, is constantly withdrawing, infinitely withdrawing, remaining other, remaining an "illeity." "Illeity is that by which the you is not the simple reverse of the I."[11]

This movement of infinition, the illeity, Levinas calls God. It is the transcendent instance that contests and judges Being. "It is the Good that calls unto Being and to expiation for the wants and faults of being."[12] Here, God is not approached through revelation but rather in the "disturbance" caused by alterity, by the Other who addresses me. In this address even my own identity is not something representative and identifiable by me. I respond with the words "here I am," enter into language, respond to alterity, bear witness to it, and in so doing do not perform an act of self-positing, but rather effect the passivity of an exposure. With these words the exposedness to the Other is shown. Through the passive expositional sense of these words witness is borne to their own unending withdrawal and transcendence. In the peculiar character of the "Here I am," witness is borne to God who is neither indicated nor named. God does not reveal himself to me, does not address me in a voice which can then become thematizable, but enters in language only in the testimony I formulate not in words which put forth my presence, but in words which expose my exposedness. The Infinite is in the command that orders me to my neighbour. Levinas sums it up as follows:

> The subjectivity of the subject, as being subject to everything, is a pre-originary susceptibility, before all freedom and outside of every present. It is accused in uneasiness of the unconditionality of the accusative, in the "here I am" (me voici) which is obedience to the glory of the Infinite that orders me to the other. 'Each of us is guilty before everyone for everyone, and I more than the others,' writes Dostoyevsky in *The Brothers Karamazov*. The subjectivity of the subject is persecution and martyrdom. It is a recurrence which is not self-consciousness, in which the subject would still be maintained distinct from itself in non-indifference, would still remain somehow in itself and be able to veil its face. This recurrence is not self-coinciding, rest, sleep or materiality. It is a recurrence on this side of oneself, prior to indifference to itself. It is a substitution for another. In the interval, it is one without attributes and not even the unity of the one doubles it up as an essential attribute. It is one absolved from every relationship every game, literally without a situation, without a dwelling place, expelled from everywhere and from itself, one saying to the other "I" of "here I am." The ego is stripped by the trauma of persecution, of its scornful and imperialist subjectivity, is reduced to the "here I am," in a transparency without opaqueness, without heavy zones propitious for evasion. "Here I am" as a witness of the infinite, but a witness that does not thematize what it bears witness to, and whose truth is not the truth of representation, is not evidence. There is a witness, a unique structure, an exception to the rule of being, irreducible to representation, only of the Infinite. The Infinite does not appear to him that bears witness to it. On the contrary the witness belongs to the glory of the Infinite. It is by the voice of the witness that the glory of the Infinite is glorified.[13]

When the Other calls upon me I can no longer avoid him, I must answer his call. The face has placed before me an inescapable choice: either I reduce the Other to my egocentric totality or I acquiesce to his pleading appeal. Whoever refuses to acquiesce to the appeal brings about evil in the strictly ethical sense of the word:

> Evil appears as sin, i.e., as the responsibility in spite of itself for the refusal to take its responsibility upon itself. One chooses for the fancy free and uncommitted irresponsibility through hurling oneself into pleasure, drink, drugs and eroticism. The distraction is the Evil. However, whoever responds positively to the Face's appeal brings about Good. One accepts the required responsibility and makes oneself available: 'here I am.'[14]

Thus the inwardness of exteriority becomes apparent. No theme, no present, has capacity for the Infinite. It is the subject who bears witness to it in the ethical bond. "The exteriority of the Infinite becomes somehow an inwardness in the sincerity of a witness born."[15] The inwardness is not a secret hidden somewhere within myself.

> It is that reverting in which the eminently exterior, precisely in virtue of this eminent exteriority, this impossibility of being contained and consequently entering into a theme, forms, as infinity, an exception to essence, concerns me and circumscribes me and orders me by my own voice. The command is stated by the mouth of him it commands. The infinitely exterior becomes an 'inward voice,' but a voice bearing witness to the fission of the inward secrecy that makes signs to another, signs of this very giving of signs.[16]

Levinas goes on to quote a Jewish proverb, "God writes straight with crooked lines."

Levinas's thought develops between his early writings and *Otherwise than Being*. If we recall chapter three on the "Trace of the Other," we remember that the Infinite was understood to have passed by having left his trace on the face of the Other. Now the Infinite passes in saying, in witness, in the command which is stated by the mouth of him it commands. However as with the trace, the Infinite passes not entering by the signification of the one-for-the-other into the being of a theme, but by signifying without thematical signification; "The saying in the said of the witness born signifies in a plot other than that which is spread out in a theme, other than that which attaches a noesis to a noema, a cause to an effect, the memorable past of the present. This plot connects to what detaches itself absolutely, to the Absolute."[17] The "here I am" is not to be held in structures of subject-object, signifier-signified, saying-said correlation. It is a sign given to the Other and in its sincerity the Infinite is glorified.

What Levinas is saying is that the Infinite has glory only through subjectivity, in the human adventure of the approach of the Other, by the expiation for the Other:

> The subject is inspired by the Infinite, which as illeity, does not appear, is not present, has always already past, is neither theme, telos nor interlocutor. It is glorified in the glory that manifests a subject, is glorified already in the glorification of its glory by the subject, thus undoing all the structures of correlation. Glorification is saying, that is, a sign given to the other, peace announced to the other, responsibility for the other, to the extent of substitution.[18]

By presenting the relationship between the Infinite and the finite in an ethical meaning Levinas does not intend to construct a "transcendental foundation" for ethical experience. There is a certain paradox here. Ethics for Levinas is beyond experience (in the phenomenological sense). It is the breakup of the originary unit of transcendental apperception. The Infinite is witnessed and not thematized. In the sign given to the Other the Infinite signifies out of responsibility for the Other a subject supporting everything and subject to everything, without having had to decide about taking this charge. "The inscription of the Other in the for-the-other of obedience is an anarchic being affected, which slips into me 'like a thief through the outstretched nets of consciousness.'"[19] Ethics conducts me into an ambiguity where the Infinite is, and which in turn makes ethics itself possible:

> It is the possibility of being the author of what has been breathed in unbeknownst to me, of having received, one knows not from where, that of which I am author. In the responsibility for the Other we are at the heart of the ambiguity of inspiration. The unheard-of saying is enigmatically in the anarchic response, in my responsibility for the Other. The trace of infinity is this ambiguity in turns beginning and makeshift, a diachronic ambivalence which ethics makes possible.[20]

Ethics leads me even beyond substitution to being a hostage for the Other. When we read Levinas, the question arises of how we can apply his insight. It is true that Levinas does not provide us with a system, nor with practical guidelines for ethics in the contemporary world. "He is first and foremost a visionary. He situates himself within his vision and invites one to share it. He presents a kind of philosophical message rather than a fully developed moral philosophy."[21] Nevertheless Levinas does believe that his moral philosophy is actually being lived out in the world around him. The following quote is a good example of this:

> One day in Louvain, after a lecture on these ideas, I was taken to a house of students (called there a "pedagogy"); I found myself surrounded by South American students, nearly all of them priests, all mainly concerned with the situation in South America. They spoke of what is happening there as a supreme test of humanity. They asked me, not without irony: where, concretely, I found the Same concerned for the Other to the point of undergoing a fission? I answered: here, at least here in a group of students and intellectuals who could very well have been pre-occupied with their inner-perfection and who have nevertheless talked of nothing but the crisis of the masses in Latin America. Were they not hostages? This utopia of conscience was historically accomplished in the room in which I found myself.[22]

Even in the smallest and most commonplace gesture, such as saying "after you" when we sit at the dinner table or walk through a door, bears witness to the ethical. If one were to reproach Levinas for his concern for the Other as being utopian, he would agree: it *is* utopian — always 'out-of-place' (u-topos) in this world, always other than the 'ways of the world.'

B) "Witness and Prophecy"

Levinas calls prophecy the reverting in which the perception of an order coincides with the signification of this order given to him that obeys it. The Other in the Same. Infinity is not announced in the witness given as a theme: "In the sign given to the Other, by which I find myself torn up from the secrecy of Gyges, 'taken by the hair' from the bottom of my obscurity, in the saying without the said of sincerity, in my 'here I am,' from the first present in the accusative, I bear witness to the Infinite."[23] The Infinite is not in front of its witness, but as it were outside or on the other side of presence, already past, out of reach – a thought behind thoughts. What Levinas is saying is that in the "here I am" the word God is still absent from the phrase in which it is being invoked. "To bear witness to God is precisely not to state this extraordinary word, as though glory would be lodged in a theme and be posited as a thesis, or become Being's essence."[24] This means that bearing witness to God is not being "occupied with God" ("Sich nicht mit Gott befassen," M. Buber) but rendering service. "Here I am" means that I in the name of God, am at the service of men that look to me, and that I am void of any self-identifying, and do not return upon myself. Bearing witness to God is an effusion of oneself, an "extraditing" of the Self to the neighbour. "Witness is humility and admission; it is made before all theology; it is kerygma and prayer, glorification and recognition."[25]

The Infinite orders me the neighbour as a face and does so without being exposed to me. The order has not been the cause of my response. I find the order in my response itself, which manifests itself as a sign given to the neighbour, as a "here I am" which brings me out of invisibility, out of the shadow in which responsibility could have been evaded. The way for this order to come to me, (although I know not from where, I know that it is non-recalling, non-phenomenal, beyond representation and affects me unbekownst to myself) "slipping into me like a thief" is what Levinas has called illeity. The third person is he in function of whom the second person eludes apprehension. The entry of the third party is not simply a multiplication of the Other, but simultaneously other than the Other. It is not the reversibility of the relationship with alterity that produced it but its multiplication to the second power. It is the entry of a third party treating me as an Other alongside of the Other I faced. The introduction of the third party is the discovery of the exigency for justice, for an order among responsibilities. "With the entry of the third party, there arises a problem of co-presence and synchronization, of distributive justice. There arises a problem of consciousness which is con-sciousness."[26] Just as the Christian, in accordance with the Gospel of St. John, pronounces "God is love," similarly Levinas, in accordance with Judaic tradition, would say, "God is justice."

Levinas is insisting that my concern for others is one based on fraternity and no on genus. The others do not affect me as examples of the same genus united with the neighbour by resemblance or common nature, as "chips off the same block." Rather it is my relationship with the other as neighbour that gives meaning to my relations with all others. All human relations must proceed from the disinterestedness, the proximity of the one-for-the-other.

"This means concretely or empirically that justice is not a legality regulating human masses, from which a technique of social equilibrium is drawn, harmonizing, antagonistic forces."[27] Justice is impossible without the-one-for-the-other substitution as its base. "Justice, society, the state and its institutions, exchanges and work are comprehended out of proximity. This means that nothing is outside of the control of the responsibility of the one for the other."[28] If there were only two of us in the world, I and the Other, there would be no problem. The Other would be my responsibility completely. But in the real world there are many Others, both distant and proximate, intimate and functional, present and absent, all of whom have relations with one another in the most differing and intricate manners. In the I-thou relation there is always the implicit presence of an absent third-party who also has a part. The injustice which I do will always have ramifications for a third party. From this it is obvious that the results of my deeds no longer coincide exactly with what they were intended to be. They reach further and receive an "objective" meaning, which is not enclosed in the subjective intentional meaning. Thus my deeds can bring about injustices which I did not intend. In this sense I can never fully take into account the Other's relation with his "Other" who is for me the third party.

Admittedly, the concept of illeity as Levinas likes to use it – often separately from a pure ethical context – could appear somewhat vague at times. For example, "The third party is other than the neighbour, but also another neighbour, and also a neighbour of the Other, and not simply his fellow."[29] Concepts such as first, second, or third person should not be first and foremost considered numerically but ethically. I myself, the Ego am rendered an "ille" by virtue of the illeity of another "ille." I am, thanks to him, one among others, someone to be concerned about, someone to answer for:

> The relationship with the third party is an incessant correction of the asymmetry of proximity in which the face is looked at. There is weighing, thought, objectification, and thus a decree in which my anarchic relationship with illeity is betrayed, but in which it is conveyed before us. There is betrayal of my anarchic relation with illeity, but also a new relationship with it; it is only thanks to God that as a subject incomparable with the other, I am approached as an other by the others. That is, "for myself." "Thanks to God" I am another for the others. God is not involved as an alleged interlocutor; the reciprocal relationship

binds me to the other man in the trace of transcendence, in illeity. The passing of God, of whom I can speak only by reference to this aid or this grace, is precisely the reverting of the incomparable subject into a member of society.[30]

On the other hand, the second person, the thou whom I am facing, is also there in virtue of an "ille," in the sense that the ille is the place from which he comes: "The beyond from whence the face comes is the third person. The pronoun ille expresses his inexpressible irreversibility... The illeity of the third person is the condition of his irreversibility."[31]

Last, but not least, illeity could also be seen as being with God, though this would be a thematization of God which Levinas is seeking to avoid; "The detachment of the Infinite from the thought that seeks to thematize it and the language that tries to hold it in the said is what we have called illeity."[32]

Levinas's use of the concept 'illeity' marks a departure from some of his contemporaries such as Martin Buber and Gabriel Marcel. Levinas does not want to use the "thou." When Gabriel Marcel speaks of an "absolute thou," Levinas sees in this a "contradiction adjecto." "Thou" signifies a relationship of familiarity and symmetry, whereas the Ab-solute, not relative or comparative, unqualified, unconditional, self-existent and conceivable without relation to other things, signifies the total dissolving, the total "Loslösung" of all relationship.

For this reason Levinas is searching for a new terminology. For Levinas, God is definitely a person, but the familiar "thou" may lead one to too easily forget the infinite transcendence of the Holy. That is why Levinas prefers the distanced "ille" when speaking about God. God is the third person, the "he," the "ille." "The untouchableness of the Infinite, His sublimeness and our irreversible relationship with Him is better expressed in the concept of illeity as in an "absolute thou.""[33] Speaking once to fellow Jews, Levinas explained: "The direct encounter with God, this is a Christian concept. As Jews, we are always a threesome: I and you and the Third who is in our midst. And only as a Third does He reveal Himself."[34]

C) "Responsibility and 'Law and Order' "

Responsibility for the Other as substitution should not bee seen as a denial of law and order. In many ways Levinas defends the lex talionis; "an eye for an eye and a tooth for a tooth." Man's responsibility is so serious, the evil one does to another cannot easily be undone, even by God. In a world where only love and tenderness would rule one runs the risk of being too passive when faced with evil. If one is too generous and forgives too easily, one takes neither the crime nor the freedom which is its source seriously enough. If one excuses sin too easily, man's autonomy is denied, as is the evil proceeding from it. "The impossibility on the part of God to forgive the offense of one man against another can be attributed not only to the fact that God does not want to upset the order of that which He has created – the law which He has left behind (because according to the law man is called to restitution for his offenses), but out of respect for man."[35] In any society, there will always be those who live the "egocentrism" and the "I." This problem has to be dealt with as Levinas explains; "regardless of the rights of love, one must always provide and keep a warm place for Hitler and his followers. Without a hell for evil, nothing in the world would have meaning any longer."[36]

It is true that Levinas's concept of substitution requires a full submission on my part towards the crimes of the Other which are committed against me. However when the offenses of the Other affect the third person, action is called for:

> If there were only the Other before me I would say that I owe him everything. I'm there for him and that even means for the evil that he inflicts upon me. I am not his equal, I'm fully subjected to him. My resistance begins when the evil which he inflicts upon me is also inflicted upon a third person who is also my neighbour. It is the third person who is the source of justice. It is the violence upon the third person that justifies the stopping the violence of the other by violent means.[37]

The idea of substitution means that I substitute myself for the Other but I cannot require of another that he substitute himself for me. This says Levinas, would be the beginning of immorality. "The I is persecuted and in principle he is responsible for the persecution inflicted upon him. However, fortunately, he is not alone. There is a third person and one cannot allow the persecution of the third person."[38]

Therefore, while the Other is in principle infinite for me, I can to a certain extent, though only to a certain extent, limit the scope of my obligations.

This means that the I can be called in the name of his unlimited responsibility to be concerned for my own affairs also.[39] If I have nothing which I can offer the Other I cannot fulfill my responsibility, I can only offer something when I have it among the "treasures" of my own self-development. Therefore I must be occupied with my own self-development in order to be able to genuinely fulfill my responsibilities. Nevertheless, any self-development has to be accomplished with regard towards helping others.

When Levinas speaks about 'the state,' what he really has in mind is a sort of universal society, which would include all of humanity. To found a state based on "people" or "nation" on a circumscribed group of people always gives rise to "nationalist" interests. This falls short of the mandate because national states always run the risk of being reduced to national egoisms. This leads to the restoration of individual totalizing egocentralism on the national scale, the war system and colonialism. The principle of universal responsibility becomes lost. Therefore national justice must be surpassed by "universal justice." The goal of universal justice is a totally human society in which all peoples are equal and no one people is exploited or oppressed by another.

> Levinas characterizes the universal human society built on the basis of an ethical brotherhood, from his own Jewish background as "messianic politics." Actually he could also just call it "messianism" since in Jewry, messianism is of itself political. The Messiah is seen as a Prince of the house of David, and his task is to bring about a just society (i.e. "peace"-"shalom") and to free humanity after he has freed Israel. Only then can God come to bring the future of eschatological world. From this perspective, therefore, Levinas can characterize the supernatural, world-wide, or "human society" as the messianic peace. Only when its peace has surpassed national particularisms and becomes the expression of universal ethical responsibility is it a true peace which no longer results from averted and fought wars but from the unconditional non-indifference of brotherhood.[40]

Notes
[1] Alphonso Lingis, "Translator's Introduction," in OBBE xii.
[2] Ibid.
[3] OBBE 135.

4. OBBE 135.
5. Lingis, xiv.
6. Ibid.
7. EI 16
8. OBBE 138.
9. Lingis, xviii.
10. Ibid.
11. Ibid.
12. Ibid.
13. OBBE 146.
14. Roger Burggraeve, "The Ethical Basis for a Humane Society," *Ephemerides Theologicae Lovanienses* 57 (1981): 27.
15. OBBE 147.
16. OBBE 147.
17. OBBE 148.
18. OBBE 148.
19. OBBE 148
20. OBBE 149.
21. Abner Weiss, "Ethics as Transcendence and the Contemporary World," in *Modern Jewish Ethics*, ed. Marvin Fox (Columbus, Ohio: Ohio State University Press, 1975), 148.
22. Levinas, *De Dieu qui vient à l'dée* (Paris: J. Vrin, 1982), 131.
23. OBBE 149.
24. OBBE 149.
25. OBBE 149.
26. Lingos, xxxvi.
27. OBBE 159.
28. OBBE 159.
29. OBBE 157.
30. DEHH 199.
31. DEHH 199.
32. OBBE 147.
33. Stefan Strasser, *Jenseits von Sein und Zeit* (The Hague: Martinus Nijhoff, 1978), 212.
34. Levinas, "Ideology and Idealism," in *Modern Jewish Ethics*, 136.

[35] Fernando Filioni, "Dio e l'alterità nel pensiero di Emmanuel Levinas," *Aquinas* 22 (1979): 67.
[36] QLT 185.
[37] Levinas, *De Dieu qui vient à l'idée,* 134.
[38] Ibid., 135.
[39] QLT 180.
[40] Burggraeve, 46.

6
Language as Prayer

Language is the obsession of a self besieged by others. — Levinas

Levinas is always seeking to develop the idea of the interior life, life perpendicular to its normal currents. Interiority, the essential element of human existence, stands on its own, outside history, outside historical time. The historical and the past are themes fixed in the past; they no longer bespeak themselves. Therefore, "the real must not only be determined in its historical objectivity, but also from interior intentions, from the secrecy that interrupts the continuity of historical time."[1] The inner life is the way in which the real can exist as plurality. The separated being of the individual is in existence quite by itself, without participating in being, from which it is separated. The soul is the part of the psyche which accomplishes this separation.

Despite the separation between beings, individuals are in a state of relation with each other. The domicile of this relation is discourse. Discourse is the primordial relation with exterior beings. Language is not an act or a gesture of human behaviour; neither is it a purely formal, mechanistic process. Far from being unattached sememes slipping from our tongues, words are transporters of life: they are the breaths that the soul takes. Language is the means by which we reach out to the Other and come to know the Other.

The essential purpose of language is interpellation. Language is oriented toward the Other. This is Levinas's original contribution to the study of language, one that is in contrast to most widely held positions. Normally, language is explained in terms of the needs or desires of the speaker. In more formalized schools of linguistics such as semantics, language is a bridge, a means of transport between the intended meaning of the speaker and the expressed text, between that which I intend to say and that which I speak. Its primary purpose is that of communication, and this act of communicating is seen as a purely mechanistic process. Semantics is concerned with the immediate meaning of communication and employs a formal method in pursuit of it. Like all forms of scientific methodology, it is a system closed within itself, drawing all of its meanings from within itself. Geoffrey Leach in his book *Semantics* affirms this:

> ... it is mistaken to try to define meaning by reducing it to the terms of sciences other than the science of language: e.g. to the terms of psychology or chemistry... meaning can best be studied as a linguistic phenomenon in its own right, not as something 'outside language.' This means we investigate what it is to 'know a language' semantically, e.g. to know what is involved in recognizing relations of meaning between sentences, and in recognizing which sentences are meaningful and which are not.[2]

Within such a conception of language there is absolutely no question of the existence of an 'Other.' The Other in the spontaneity of his exteriority does not even enter into the field of perception of semantics. There is no such thing as speaking for "the sake of another." Speaking is always for my own sake. Semantics is a form of structuralism — an attempt to give a structured, systematic, and totalizing explanation of language.

In semiotics notions about language are not as strict. Language exists primarily for the sake of the speaker. Language is seen as a means of situating oneself in the world (*un se situer dans le monde, un se situer dans son être*), a tool for coming to grips with the world. Representatives of this tradition, such as Algirdas Greimas, say the purpose of language is not communication, as with semantics, but manipulation in a positive sense.[3] The goal of speaking is inevitably to "convince" the Other (playing on the Latin *con vincere,* to conquer). When I succeed in convincing someone, I have conquered him, pulled him over to my side, made him see my way of seeing things. The Other is integrated into the same.

Levinas is strongly opposed to both of these ways of treating language. Language is for him neither solely a vehicle of communication nor a means of manipulation. It is a phenomenon which is 'beyond all systems,' a revelation:

> The communication of ideas, the reciprocity of dialogue, already hide
> the profound essence of language. It resides in the irreversibility of the
> relation between me and the Other, in the Mastery of the Master
> coinciding with his position as other and as exterior. For language can
> be spoken only if the interlocution is the commencement of the
> discourse; if consequently, he remains beyond the system, if he is not
> on the same plane as myself. The interlocutor is not a Thou, he is a You
> (*Il n'est pas un Tu, il est un Vous*); he reveals himself in his lordship.
> This exteriority coincides with a mastery. My freedom is challenged by
> a Master who can invest it.[4]

For Levinas, language is first and foremost at the service of the one being addressed. I begin to speak not just for my own sake, nor to make myself feel more at ease, but for the sake of the Other in order that he may feel more at ease; language is likened to politeness. Real communication takes place in the silence before speech. When I speak, I am being polite. I am interpreting to the Other what I have already communicated to him. I am putting him at ease; to remain silent would be too rude. It would lead to discomfort, sometimes horror. Continued silence would be the inverse of language. "The interlocutor has given a sign, but has declined every interpretation; this is the silence that terrifies."[5] It is the bewitched world, the mythological, the mystical, occult world that remains silent. Speech is an ever-renewed promise to clarify what was obscure. Language, in its essence, creates closeness with another human being. An example which Levinas gives is that of two strangers sitting across from each other in a train, not speaking to one another, an uneasy air between them. Once they begin speaking, things reverse themselves: the ice is broken and both begin to feel more at ease. Even when words for one another are harsh the effect is better than no exchange of words at all. "The claim to know and to reach the Other is realized in the relationship with the Other that is cast in the relation of language, where the essential is the interpellation, the vocative."[6]

In addressing the Other, I am affirming him in his being. I am showing respect for him, acknowledging his existence. When I call upon the Other to speak, I am calling for his assistance; in calling for his assistance, I am calling on him to be present, to present life, to present himself.

Language is a giving, a giving of myself over to others. Language is that which creates community and universality because it is the passage between one individual and another. "Language does not refer to the generality of concepts, but lays the foundations for a possession in common... it is what I give: the communicable, the thought, the universal."[7] Language is an ethical event: to speak is to make the world common, to create commonplaces. Speech is a primordial disposition in which a thing becomes a thing for everybody.

Language resists totalization; speech brings an inexhaustible surplus of attention to the relation to the Other. With its infinite number of possible combinations, language is directly reflective of Infinity, even a manifestation thereof. I am taught and formed through Infinity disclosed in language, disclosed in my encounter with the Other. And like the Other, language does not allow itself to be fully analyzed, fully formalized, fully represented in semantic meaning, as with text models. Language cannot be reduced to a system of signs. It is the excrescence of the word. A word, though carrying concreteness and temporalization, transcends itself, transports us to the hither side of the said. Language permits us to go outside of Being, outside the theme in which Being has already been placed.

Language may be likened not merely to politeness but even to supplication, to prayer. Language holds one in place, as it were. It is putting myself before the Other in respect and attention, in reverence and vigilance. It is a pleading of the Other who is always above me.

> He who speaks to me and across the words, proposes himself to me, retains the fundamental foreignness of the Other who judges me; our relations are never reversible. According to the distinction established by Plato in the Phaedrus, discourse is discourse with God and not with equals. The essence of this discourse with him who is above me, with God, leaks beyond being. It is metaphysics. Language is metaphysics and thus a prayer, like attentiveness, a beseeching, a vigilance.[8]

Levinas writes about the "conversational situation between two people." He is not interested in the subject-object relationship of grammar — this is not metaphysics: what interests him is the dynamic of the situation itself, one person disclosing himself to another. The conversational situation is not the same as an epistemological situation: the object of knowledge in an epistemological situation is a fact, finished and belonging to the past; the one appealed to in conversation is called to answer, to speak, and is subsequently made present. The spoken word is more than a simple sign: it teaches. It comes from a teacher.

Language is where the face to face encounter takes place. It is not a game, by no means a Wittgensteinian *Sprachspiel*. Before all the linguistic systems and formalizations there is the pre-original *lieu* : the proximity of the one to the Other; the commitment of the one to the Other; the substitution of the one for the Other. Levinas explains that Spinoza's understanding of existence is that to be is to persevere in one's being (*être, c'est persister dans son être.*). Being is the effort of being. It is a struggle. But there is a break in this effort as soon as I encounter the Other. I have a responsibility to go out of myself and over to the Other; and the first instance of this is when I simply say "hello," "*bonjour:*" The hello is the first religious miracle, the first religious moment:

> Should language be thought of solely as the communication of an idea, or of information, and not above all else, as the fact of approaching the Other as Other, that is to say, answering him? Is not the first word 'hello' (*bonjour*)! Simply hello... hello as a blessing and as my availability for another person. This does not yet mean "what a nice day" (*quelle belle journée*). This means, I wish you peace, I wish you a good day. It is the expression of him who cares for another. It carries all the remainder of the conversation. It carries the entire discourse.[9]

We have looked at language under its positive qualities as something that consoles and expresses reverence. But what happens when words become brutal or malicious? When they are spoken not to instruct but rather to deceive? Levinas is well aware of this problem, and writes:

> The human being is characterized as human not only because he is a being who can speak, but also because he is a being who can lie, who can live in the duplicity of language as the dual possibility of exposure and deception. The animal is incapable of this duplicity; the dog, for instance, cannot suppress its bark, the bird its song. But man can suppress his saying, and this ability to keep silent, to withhold oneself, is the ability to be political.[10]

Here Levinas makes a distinction between saying (*le dire*) and the said (*le dit*). Language understood as saying is language as exposure, as ethical openness to the Other. The said is a totalizing closure; the saying is that which keeps language alive. The said is what freezes the message into place. There is no life within the said. The task of philosophy is to keep the saying alive.

In *Otherwise Than Being or Beyond Essence*, Levinas embarks upon the audacious task of reducing the said to the saying and turning language into a "performing that never rounds off in a finished performance." The passages in *Otherwise than Being or Beyond Essence* concerning this reduction are extremely complex, at times even more difficult to follow than Levinas's explanations of the Trace. For example, Levinas describes the word in its interplay between the saying and the said as:

> ... an obedience in the midst of the will ('I hear this or that said'), a kerygma at the bottom of a fiat. Before all receptivity an already said before languages exposes or, in all the sense of the term, signifies (proposes and orders) experience, giving to historical languages spoken by peoples a locus, enabling them to orient or polarize the diversity of the thematized as they choose.[11]

This is in line with Levinas's reflections on the Idea of the Infinite and the Other: as the Other always exceeds any idea we may form about him, so language always exceeds its own formulations. What we want to say is rarely expressed satisfactorily in the words we use to say it: we do not find the right words! As the Infinite exceeds its own idea, so saying is conceived as a surplus over evidence, theme, and logic.[12] In the saying there is always more than in the said. It is to the saying, therefore, that we should maintain an openness. Levinas wants us to remain open toward the Other in order to be respondent to his vitality and spontaneity, and not to trap him in sociological and psychological analyses and theories. Levinas beseeches us to maintain an openness toward language, to see language as something young and fresh, not fossilized in dead, absolute sentences and theories. As the Other is not a threatening shadow, neither is language a "verbal" intruder waiting to trick us: rather it soothes, consoles, and creates closeness. *Language* and *languish* have no common root.

The problem of maliciousness and deception in language is directly linked to the problem of evil in the Other. Language can deceive me just as the Other can inflict injustice upon me. Yet his misdeeds do not make up his essence. Once executed, they are dead facts of the past. The real essence is above the facts, transcendental. It lies simply in his being the Other, an infinitesimal opening, a revelation, fundamentally a friend rather than a foe. Levinas would have us realize that, similarly, the essence of language is not in the said, be it harsh or kind, false or true. The essence of language is above words. It is in the "positive production of the infinite," and in the resultant closeness with the Other: "The essence of language is hospitality, goodness."[13]

Levinas calls saying a passivity, not "as arising from the impact of objects striking an inert mental apparatus waiting to be awakened,"[14] but as an upsurge: language is one of the ways in which being manifests itself. Languages elicit and bring things forth into full presence. Passivity in saying is the basic passivity of the one for the Other. Saying does not proclaim its own formulations "ex cathedra" and impose them upon the Other. Saying is being at the service of the Other, a showing of myself to the Other, the renunciation of all secrecy:

> Saying is this passivity of passivity and this dedication to the Other, this sincerity. Not the communication of a said, which would immediately cover over and extinguish or absolve the said, but saying holding open to its openness, without excuses, evasions or alibis, delivering itself without saying anything said. Saying saying saying itself, without thematizing it, but exposing it again... It is to exhaust oneself in exposing oneself, to make signs by making oneself a sign, without resting in one's every figure as a sign. In the passivity of the obsidional extradition, this very extradition is delivered over to the Other, before it could be established. This is the pre-reflexive iteration of the saying of this very saying, a statement of the "here I am".[15]

Levinas has attempted to analyze language beyond its communicative qualities. He is not concerned with verifying the truth of the information it carries. Unlike Buber, Levinas does not found language upon any distinction between authentic or inauthentic speech. What he wants to show is the proximity contained within language. The occasionally excruciating phenomenological rigour of his investigations notwithstanding, his basic notion of language is an unscientific one. It is seen in the interhuman realm, not the scientific or experimental. The meaning of speech goes well beyond grammatical or semantic models. Speech is never purely subjective, words are not turned back to the speaking subject, as in psychoanalysis, but are always addressed to another. Speech is always intersubjective, dialogical, never solely a monologue with oneself.

Psycholinguists have for sometime now affirmed that madness is directly linked to language, to the inability to express oneself verbally. Madness is also the most solitary of diseases because relationships with other human beings are impossible without the ability to converse coherently with them. The words of the schizophrenic are not addressed to Others but to voices within his own head. This may be an instance of purely subjective speech, or the result of it.

Levinas's notion of language is biblical. Words are holy. I have to listen. They vow me to the Other: 'Thou shalt not kill; Thou shalt love thy neighbour as thine own self...' When it is I who pronounce them, they become a supplication — a prayer.

Notes:

[1] TI 58

[2] Geoffrey Leech, *Semantics*. (Great Britain: Penguin Books, 1985), 8.

[3] Algirdas Julien Greimas, *Du sens*. (Paris: Editions du Seuil, 1970).

[4] TI 106.

[5] TI 91.

[6] TI 69.

[7] TI 97.

[8] OBBE 5.

[9] OBBE 92.

[10] "Dialogue with Emmanuel Levinas," interview by Richard Kearney, in *Face to Face with Levinas*, ed. Richard Cohen (Albany: State University of New York Press, 1986), 29.

[11] OBBE 36.

[12] Steven G. Smith, "Reason as One for Another: Moral and Theoretical Argument," in *Face to Face with Levinas*, 62.

[13] TI 174.

[14] Edith Wyschogrod, *Emmanuel Levinas. The problem of Ethical Metaphysics.* (The Hague: Martinus Nijhoff, 1974), 131.

[15] OBBE 143.

PART II

Emmanuel Levinas in Perspective

7
An Excessive Ethics

If we think of Levinas's view of the human being as a responsible self, we can see that there is a good reason to place Levinas in the Kantian tradition. Levinas certainly has an affinity for Kant and appears to consider Kant's separation of morality from ontology to be the German's greatest achievement in ethics:

> If one had the right to retain one trait from a philosophical system and neglect all the details of its architecture...we would think here of Kantianism, which finds a meaning to the human without measuring it by ontology and outside of the question "What is there here...?" that one would like to take to be preliminary, outside of the immortality and death which ontologies run up against. The fact that immortality and theology could not determine the categorical imperative signifies the novelty of the Copernican revolution: a sense that is not measured by being or not being; but being on the contrary is determined on the basis of sense.[1]

Levinas, as Kant before him, wants to emphasize the precedence of practical over theoretical reason.

Levinas's notion of responsibility certainly resembles Kant's notion of the moral imperative. Similarly, as access to the realm of the transcendent leads by way of ethics for Levinas, so too for Kant, God is a postulate of moral reason (but just a postulate). However, unlike the Kantian moral deduction, "...God is not attained in the demand for moral intelligibility that postulates Him, for the demand for certainty and even for articulation in the coherent text of the said already deforms His witness."[2]

Kant claims that actions are morally good only when performed for the sake of duty. In the following chapter, where we will examine the influence of Judaic traditions upon the thought of Levinas, it will become evident that he believes that moral behaviour rests on obedience to the law as found in the Torah. The difference between the two thinkers is that Kant's duty is a product of moral reason based upon a formal principle or maxim — which is in turn a purely personal, subjective principle upon which we act while, for Levinas, it is the result of a combination of divine revelation and human inclination. Even the appealing face of the Other is a sort of revelation, the living word of God. Furthermore, Kant says that we must obeys all laws for their own sake. In Levinas, we shall obey the law for the sake of the Other, and one could even say, that the law issues from the Other.

Speaking in phenomenological terms and leaving the law aside for the moment, we can see that Levinas detaches reason altogether from the moral self. Levinas does not agree with Kant's conception of inclination and duty. According to Kant, if we base our actions upon maxims grounded in inclination rather than in duty, we have failed to act in accordance with the moral law. Kant subordinates inclination to reason. For Levinas, however, what is moral cannot be sought as in Kant, "a priori," simply in the conception of pure reason. In Levinas, duty results from inclination in terms of affect. "Affect is no longer, as it was for Kant, at best an incidental but unwarranted intrusion upon the ground of maxims, sullying the purity of an otherwise moral act and, at worst, upsetting in its very upsurge, the possibility of moral action itself. Affectivity in Levinas's thought becomes the lived mode of morality."[3] There is an affectivity and an inclination which is expressed as an instinctive attachment to the good and which Levinas has termed desire, as already treated in chapter four.

Kant thought that the will was autonomous because it could legislate universal maxims for itself based on reason alone. If the will was heteronomous (that is to say determined by forces outside of itself, such as the causal laws of nature), then it could not give us truly moral laws, since it would be too concerned with results, and with moral actions as mere means to these desired ends. This would destroy all immediate interest in moral action and place man under the laws of nature, rather than the reason-based law of freedom. By showing the difference between the phenomenal world (of nature and appearance) and the noumenal world (of human reason) Kant is able to preserve a realm of human freedom in the post-Newtonian world of total natural causality.

Levinas sees Husserl as having found a way to heal the rift between the noumenal and phenomenal spheres, for Husserl was able to show that we can intuit values directly, in the same way we do other essences. For Husserl, man's values lie once again within the ontological sphere. Therefore we have moral values within the ontological sphere. But this is still not good enough. Moral values still arise in the phenomenal realm but are now borne by persons and are intuited in the very appearance of these persons as being of transcendental origin. Moral action is not founded in a universal principle worked out by reason:

> My responsibility for the other man, the paradoxical, contradictory responsibility for a foreign liberty — extending, according to the Talmud (Sotah 37b), even to responsibility for his responsibility — does not originate in a vow to respect the universality of a principle, nor in a moral imperative. It is the exceptional relation in which the Same can be concerned with the Other, without the Other's being assimilated to the Same, the relation in which one can recognize the inspiration in the strict sense of the term, to bestow spirit upon man.[4]

Levinas insists that the will is heteronomous. The moral self is to itself its own egoity, but it remains strictly dependent upon other persons:

> The Other is one's teacher; his transcendence guarantees the moral self. Levinas remains Kantian in insisting upon the immediate and apodictive upsurge of value and in rejecting an empirical foundation for the moral self. Yet we have seen that the Other appears as phenomenon, is a unique given who breaks through the form of his appearance to become a transcendent source of value. Thus, while the moral self does not need the presented world insofar as it can be represented, it is subjected to the presented when what is presented is the other person who is the source of all moral value.[5]

We see then the laudability of Levinas's attempt to form an ethics of obligation while avoiding the traditional Kantian extreme of individualism, by holding that it is ultimately the individual who decides rationally where his priorities and obligations lie. In everyday life we do not always have the luxury to sit back leisurely and rationally to plan out our ethical behaviour: the numerous daily commitments and sacrifices we must constantly make do not always lend themselves to individual analysis. There are responsibilities and obligations, duty to be done. It would be moral schizophrenia to explain our behaviour purely on rational or utilitarian grounds.

This is plain and simple on a 'straightforward' human level, but philosophers are rarely satisfied with the plain and simple, and Levinas is no exception. It is with his sophistication here that the usual tangles in moral philosophy today begin to surface.

Levinas insists on the priority of ethics over ontology, and calls upon Plato to demonstrate the first evidence of this priority: "In Greek philosophy one can already discern traces of the ethical breaking through the ontological, for example in Plato's idea of the 'good existing beyond being' (agathon epekeina tes ousias)."[6] Plato does not understand the idea of the 'good existing beyond being' as does Levinas. For Levinas "the good," or ethical principles, are inseparable from human sociality and action. Plato's approach is conceptualist. Plato believed there was an independent principle at work in human actions which could not be deduced from the experiences of daily life, nor to the utilitarian ends of pleasure or usefulness.

If a man kills another he may feel a sense of satisfaction — he has rid himself of a rival, perhaps, or may profit from the deed by seizing the other's wealth or throne. The wrong done to the deceased may not itself make the deed evil — the soul of the victim may after all have flown from its earthly vale of tears to the Elysian Field, benefitting from the event; yet evil has been done, and no power in the world can change this.[7] This is one of the puzzles in Levinas's argument. When arguing a position, he often introduces examples or comparisons which in themselves suggest a position totally opposed to his own. He calls Western thought an *egologie*, for example, and then brings in Descartes — of all people — as an exception to the rule! In the realm of ethics he makes cross references, such as that to Plato above, which, when taken in their own context, are arguments against his position. A common criticism of Levinas in this regard is that he is too indebted to the very system he rejects.

Levinas describes his ethics not as an ideology, but as an idealism, and, like all forms of idealism, its attractiveness is also its weakest point. His basic claim is that we all possess within ourselves a feeling of responsibility for others. Through a very complex phenomenological investigation of various facets of human life, he argues that there is much evidence of people living altruistically; a mother making immeasurable sacrifices for her children, the soldier who throws himself upon a grenade to save the lives of his comrades. But this is nothing new. Many standard 'Philosophical Theories of God' use the argument of 'a consciousness of moral obligation' to give 'proofs' for the existence of God. Such theories hold it to be a fact that we all make moral judgements, that we all have a sense of right and wrong: we may be impressed by the ingeniousness of a bank robbery, but still we condemn the action as being wrong. We all have certain innate values and consequently feel compelled to live according to these values. For if we do not, we suffer from a sense of guilt. The next question is, where do these values come from? There must be a source, and this source has to be a higher power, outside of ourselves, to have instilled us with these values. The proponents of such theories argue that moral obligation is first and foremost towards individual persons and can stem only from them. Thus all sociological theories of collective moral consciousness are dispelled. This higher power has also to be a person: obviously not a person in the sense that all human beings are, but rather that it has the qualities of a person within itself, — namely a personal God.

Levinas's thinking follows this scheme in essence, the main difference being that this higher power, having the qualities of a person and being the ultimate source of my 'feeling of obligation,' does not seem to be any different from the Other to whom I am obligated. In a sense, the Other is elevated to the status of God. Time after time Levinas refers to the Other as "He who is above me, He who is higher up." In most cases he writes Other with a capital letter (l'Autre). The ethics of Levinas is an excessive ethics; excessive alterity, excessive passivity, excessive responsibility.[8] Indeed, the problem with Levinas's asymmetrical relation to the Other , my total indebtedness to the Other with no reciprocity, is that the Other is like a God to me. Other religious writers, such as Kierkegaard, have avoided these problems by keeping ethics and religion distinct. Levinas borrows Keirkegaardian religious categories and adds the social, though for Kierkegaard these categories were essentially non-social. The writings of the mystics, whether of St. Augustine or of Theresa of Avila, are also without the social. In mysticism it is the immortality of the soul which is the basis of spirituality. For Levinas, the basis of spirituality is ethics and sociality.

Again, Levinas's "idealism instead of ideology" is attractive in that wherein it is weak. It would be wonderful to be able to believe that all men carry within themselves a feeling of responsibility for others, but there is too much evidence to the contrary. We could pore through phenomenological or psychological investigations for reassurance, but more than likely we have already seen in others if not within ourselves, that egoism, oppression and abuse are just as abundant as goodness. Perhaps it lies in our perspective on life: "I am my brother's keeper," it is said, and yet Cain rose up and slew his brother Abel.

There is a short chapter in Lev Shestov's book *Potestas Clavium* entitled "Responsibility," in which Shestov argues that all men cannot possess a common sense of responsibility because not all men see eye to eye. Both Dostoyevsky and Tolstoy, writes Shestov, meditated painfully on Napoleon. They could not understand how Napoleon could take upon himself the responsibility for all the suffering and misery he caused. They reasoned that if we sin or do injury to someone, we can no longer sleep at night. But how could Napoleon sleep at night — Napoleon, who destroyed thousands of lives daily and threatened the existence of many nations, his own among them? Dostoyevsky and Tolstoy believed that all men are constructed in the same way; if their consciences torment them, then Napoleon's ought to have caused him more suffering than most.

Shestov replies that for Napoleon the question of responsibility did not even exist: 'he lived and acted according to nature as the Stoics demanded.' Shestov continues, "it is only rarely that two men will ever come to mutually understand each other."

> The biblical story about confusion of tongues is not a fairy tale or myth, as learned people in their arrogance imagine. Even when men pronounce the same words they each mean and see different things. Two orthodox Moslems swear in the name of two different Allahs.[9]

Principles of identity only exist in logic; 'to one who thinks that responsibility is the consciousness of a moral principle that lives in the heart of each of us it is not given to 'understand' Napoleon.' Shestov concludes by saying, that the majority of men of action have been 'irresponsible,' for "one who takes upon himself responsibility, if he be not God but a man, paralyzes in himself the nerve of action and condemns himself to idleness and reflection."[10] This is the role of the philosopher. But when the philosopher begins to act, he too becomes irresponsible because he can never know what will come of his deeds, even in empirical reality.

Levinas understands this well himself, and says that we are infinitely responsible for the unforeseeable repercussions of our actions, there is no limit to our responsibility. What then should we do? Should we vow ourselves to silence, put a limit on our thinking and remain idle? Levinas does not follow these questions through.

To return to Shestov, what some believe to be good and just, others may not, and vice versa. The Western world may condemn terrorism but in other cultures it is seen as a justified means to achieve one's end or make one's cause known. Western man may abhor the thought of war while for others war can be holy, a religious duty. We may be against discrimination on the grounds of race, creed or nationality, but in every nationalistic movement discrimination on the grounds of nationality is at the forefront.

Could Levinas be saying that we should at least attempt to live according to what we hold to be true and right? If so, will it bring us any closer to the "utopos" of which he speaks? Can it solve the conflict in values which exists among men? Levinas wants unlimited respect for the Other to be the basis of our ethical behaviour: I have no right to harm or halt the Other; the only time I can interfere with the activity of the Other is when I see him harming a third. Alas, this only brings us full circle. One party sees another doing harm to a third and intervenes to stop the second, but the second initially acted because it believed the third to be allied with the first and threatening a fourth, and so on.

Being responsible for others is a beautiful ideal, one that we can accept as a fact of life, believe in in the light of faith in God, or work out for ourselves by some personal utilitarian, sociological or phenomenological discovery. Levinas has attempted to show that we instinctively act responsibly towards others. But to say that we feel a sense of responsibility towards others as an innate, essential part of our being is excessive: Some may feel it, others do not; some serve, others plunder.

Notes

[1] OBBE 129.
[2] Alphonso Lingis, "Translator's Introduction," in OBBE xxv.
[3] Edith Wyschogrod, *Emmanuel Levinas: The Problem of Ethical Metaphysics* (The Hague: Martinus Nijhoff, 1974), 208.
[4] Levinas, "Ideology and Idealism," in *Modern Jewish Ethics*, ed. Marvin Fox (Columbus, Ohio: State University Press, 1975), 135.
[5] Wyschogrod, 135.

[6] "Dialogue with Emmanuel Levinas," interview by Richard Kearney, in *Face to Face with Levinas*, ed. Richard Cohen (Albany: State University of New York Press, 1986), 25.

[7] Lev Shestov, *Potestas Clavium*, trans. Bernard Martin (Athens, Ohio: Ohio University Press, 1968), 310f.

[8] Richard Cohen, *Face to Face with Levinas*, 8.

[9] Shestov, 165.

[10] Ibid.

8
Levinas's Critique of Martin Heidegger

Levinas, like so many others, has no doubt been greatly influenced by Martin Heidegger. He calls Heidegger's *Sein und Zeit* (Being and Time) one of the most beautiful books ever written in philosophy. His critique of Heidegger in *En découvrant l'existence avec Husserl et Heidegger* is very thorough and even favourable. Heidegger's attempt to go beyond traditional ontology has inspired Levinas, along with his amazingly perceptive work on etymologies, which always begins with the ordinary meaning of the term and then goes on to disclose an entire range of concentrated experiences.[1] Nevertheless, for Levinas the Jewish ethicist, there are certain things Heidegger does that are unforgivable. "One can forgive many Germans (the reference is in regard to Heidegger's involvement with the Nazis), but there are Germans whom it is very difficult to forgive. It is very difficult to forgive Heidegger."[2] Levinas in his critique of Heidegger feels compelled to expose the latter as an idolatrous pagan.

Martin Heidegger wants to break out of the circle of Western thinking, but according to Levinas, he remains ever so much in it. From *Sein und Zeit* onward, Heidegger sees it as his primary task to overthrow the metaphysical and scientific traditions which have predominated in Western thought ever since Plato and Aristotle. For Plato the Being of beings resided in the eternal, immutable designs of perfect form or "ideas"; for Aristotle, in "energeia," the unfolding actuality that realizes itself in substance. Plato engendered all of metaphysics right up to and including Nietzsche, and Aristotle with his investigations of first causes and dynamic principles has laid the foundations for science and technology.

Heidegger maintains that these two traditions have not developed from a genuine perception of Being, but from a forgetting of Being, from a taking for granted this central mystery of existence. Even more seriously, Heidegger also claims that this metaphysical-scientific way of looking at the world is what is responsible for the alienation of modern man, and for the barbaric state of modern technology and mass consumption in which he lives. Heidegger's principal purpose consists of a reexamination of the notion of Being and Being's relation to time. What is Being? Heidegger begins by making a distinction between the being of the existent (das Seiende) and the Being of the existent (das Sein des Seienden). It is by virtue of the latter that everything is. Being is not to be identified with any one existent, and so in a certain sense Being "is not," as it would be an existent if it were. Being is rather the event of being of all other existents. In traditional ontology this Being of existents was always identified with the Absolute or God. Heidegger, however, does not make such an identification, but does maintain that the Being of existants is the object of ontology.

Since Being is not an existent, it is not to be classified "per genus et differentiam specificam," but rather comprehended as the most fundamental characteristic of human existence. The comprehension of Being is the drama of human existence.

Heidegger maintains not merely that time is a framework of human existence, but that the "temporalization" of time is the comprehension of Being. The essence of man is his existence, the fact that he is "there." That which man is is his manner of being, and in "being there" he temporalizes himself. In a certain sense, then, Being and time are one.

In equating essence and existence, Heidegger has no intention of applying the ontological argument to man: the essence of man is not necessarily to exist , because man is not a necessary being. Rather, man's essence is included in his existence, and all essential determinations he may possess are but ways of existing. Thus Heidegger applies the word "Dasein" (being there) to man and not "Daseiendes" (the existent there). Every element of the essence of man is a way of existing, of finding oneself simply "there."

An important point regarding the above, and one on which Levinas bases much of his criticism, is that Heidegger's ontology is not interested in man as such, but in Being in general. Being has to reveal itself in order to make itself accessible. Man placed within an "économie de l'être," becomes the "lieu" of the revelation of Being. Comprehending Being is the study of the "way of being" of man; the analysis of Dasein, of "being there." The richness and diversity of human existence serves to reveal Being.

The phenomena of the world, or, more precisely, the structure of being-in-the-world is the vehicle by which the comprehension of Being is realized. Here we come to the concepts of "Vorhandenheit" and "Zuhandenheit." Dasein is a being-in-the-world — i.e., being in an environment, amongst "things." These things receive their being through being in function of Dasein (tools of Dasein); this is their Zuhandenheit, their "readiness-to-hand." Vorhandenheit is simply their presence (presentness-at-hand).

The structure of Zuhandenheit is constituted by its nature of referral (Verweisung). A tool "is for" something: a shoe is to be worn, a watch for telling time. At the same time a tool is also "for someone," for a user. They are all in function of something else. We understand these referrals when we understand the structure of Dasein, which is in function of itself, and in which these referrals take place. Zuhandenheit is the way of existing of these tools; Dasein, however, discovers its existence by virtue of itself. Dasein understands its existence to be in function of itself. At the same time, it is the initial existence in virtue of which other things have their readiness (Zuhandenheit).

One might say, then, that being for Dasein is to comprehend Being, and at the same time, a "marching forward" out into existence: "being there," in the sense of "going out there" and being-in-the-world (which Heidegger also calls Geworfenheit). This, says Levinas, is Heidegger's innovativeness: he introduces a Dasein which comprehends its own possibilities of existence and its own existence, discovering the tools of this world – knowledge formed by existence itself.

But in its strength also lies its weakness: instead of keeping its fundamental possibilities in sight, such as that of being in the world by virtue of itself, Dasein is disturbed by its own finiteness and becomes preoccupied (die Angst); it wants to flee the world. Dasein begins to comprehend itself, to find its meaning in relation to secondary things – e.g., its relative possibilities regarding the things of this world. This is Dasein's cadence (Verfallen). Dasein flees its authentic existence and falls back into daily existence (Alltäglichkeit).

However, in its weakness is also its strength: Dasein, fallen into the mundane world of objects, into dark nothingness, does not lose its character of being-in-the-world. "Much to the contrary, anguish (die Angst) delivers Dasein to the world — in as much as it is world — to the possibility of being in virtue of itself, and only allows it to attach itself to the world in as much as this world is just a collection of things, usable tools."[3] In anguish, Dasein again becomes aware of the authenticity of its existence. Dasein's "wofür" becomes identical with its "worum": to-be-in-the-world. Anguish, then, is also comprehension, the comprehension of the possibility of authentic existence.

With Heidegger the soul is not banished in the world, contrary to any platonic conception. An obscure contact with reality and all of its powers — its hostility; its weight upon one's shoulders, from which one attempts to escape – for Heidegger this is comprehension (Verstehen), and the pivot upon which all of philosophy turns. Comprehension is a movement, a route of access, a movement of the spirit, a forward movement. All ontological knowledge – that is to say, all true comprehension – is directed towards no specific object, but rather the horizon on which all objects become apparent. This horizon is the verb "to be." The comprehension of Being, then, is the supreme condition of the comprehension of all other existents.

Here again Levinas objects to Heidegger:

> Let us suppose that, that which I am, a human being, everything I do, all that which I think, are ways of comprehending the powers of Being to which I am avowed. Existence for a human being is always a relationship to his powers of Being... Man exists in virtue of his existence.[4]

Thinking is no longer a relationship between a free subject and the object which he intends to understand. Levinas asks: 'Is this then not a form of oppression?' Does this not give a totally new meaning (sens) to life? Along these lines Levinas's critique of Heidegger proceeds:

> It seems to us that one of the essential ideas of Heidegger's thought is that aside from practical, theoretical and emotional matters, which we are able to maintain with things and persons, we also maintain, by virtue of our existence, a constant relationship with the verb "to be" (être). To make one's mark upon existence is not to make use of time by way of our conscience, our thoughts, our acts and our feelings, but rather it is by fulfilling a preliminary, irreducible relationship called ontology.[5]

Levinas asks what it is to be, the central question of ontology and of all philosophy. Our purpose in life is to search for that which we already possess. Yet this is not to be confused with Plato's Menon, for in this regard Heideggerian thought is quite anti-platonic: there is no necessity here to affirm oneself as a free self who finds all within himself. All initiatives are subordinated to the anticipated realization of potential. To be a human being means basically to have *to be*, always to ask oneself what it means to be.

Transcendence in Heidegger is Dasein, the Dasein which is already there. The "Da" is its distinguishing feature. Dasein is what forms our ontological notion of the world. Dasein is not the sum of existents; rathers its way of existing comprehends existence and allows all other things to come into existence upon its horizon.

The philosophy of Heidegger renews the grand tradition of ancient philosophy, posing the question of Being as such, and at the same time provides an answer for modern thought, which has attempted to present the person as master of his own destiny. The difference is that now the sovereignty of the "I" has been separated from the Transcendent, traditionally either God or the Absolute. The philosophy of Heidegger is an attempt to present the individual as a locus where the comprehension of Being takes place, and this without any recourse to an "Eternal Being." In Being-unto-death – death being the condition of all being — the individual discovers the nothingness upon which he rests, and consequently that he rests upon nothing but himself. The structure of Dasein is not possible apart from the picture of death. This idea is found in the tradition of the "memorio mortis," from St. Augustine to Theresa of Avila.

Levinas's greatest objection to Heidegger's philosophy is that it is not interested in man as such, but first and foremost in Being – and again, not the existent (das Seiendes), but Being (das Sein). Truth is not something added to Being, resulting from man's actions; truth is the truth of Being. Man finds himself within a certain condition and there is simply no exit.

At least in idealism, says Levinas, the dignity of man is still maintained. There is no attempt made to equate the spirit of man with material existence: "Idealism refutes all common measure between the spirit and things... By affirming the anterior quality of the spirit in relation to things, idealism is, in the end event, a doctrine of human dignity."[6]

In idealism reason is still honoured. Man is not seen as a mere "principal character," produced by experience and in function of experience, but rather as one who must rely upon his own wits, upon his own faculty of reason to construct his world. It is man himself who is the point of departure; he still has control over his own destiny respective of his situation before the ideal. Levinas says that this is lacking in Heidegger, that there man is forced, even subsumed into the "ontological powers." With Heidegger's Geworfenheit a limit is placed upon intellectual activity. Idealistic consciousness is transformed into existence. The world receives meaning from man but man himself is lacking in meaning: "... Does not the novelty of Heidegger consist of subordinating the power of thought as professed in idealism to ontological conditions; to show that it is Being which forms consciousness...?"[7]

Levinas's question is this: is man's relationship with Being a purely ontological one? Is human existence realized only under the dominance of Being? In Heidegger, unfortunately, it seems to be so. And yet Heidegger is far from being the only culprit. This has been the tendency of Western philosophy since Socrates, and Heidegger should not be fooling himself – he is right in line with this tradition!

Both Levinas and Heidegger took on the phenomenological vocation to renew the life of the spirit. For Heidegger the main question is that of Being – i.e., "why is there something rather than nothing?" This question instantiates self-being as the source of meaning and value, and Heidegger assures us, will lead us back to the revelation (alethea) of Being, by returning us to the origin of revelation in the pasture lands of pre-Socratic paganism.[8] For Levinas the main question is that of "infinity" – i.e., "why am I nothing rather than something?" This question goes beyond self-being, to discover in the Other the source of meaning and value; it does not lead us back to some 'place," some 'Ithaca' (Heidegger's pre-Socratic topos), but forward, to a 'no-place' (u-topos).

Revelation for Heidegger means settlement, taking up a position and putting down roots, Da-sein; for Levinas it means unsettlement, disposition, a pulling up of roots. Levinas's image of man is Mosaic man, man who journeys outwards in search of an ideal justice with the Other. This image is in sharp contrast to that of man in the pre-Socratic pastureland, drawn towards a centre by a kind of ontological gravity; the gravity creating a totality by drawing all beings to itself,[9] all beings participating in this overall 'totality' of Being. Levinas denounces this notion of a single Being totalizing multiple beings: "Beings are invaded by the chaotic unfolding of anonymous Being, that horrible neutrality."[10] Levinas is attacking not only

Heidegger but Western philosophy also, and precisely because it is ontological: "Western philosophy is an ontology; it is therefore incapable of talking about transcendence. It transforms not only God, but also human beings, even the thinking subject himself is transformed into moments or 'adventures' of Being."[11] Levinas proposes to replace this monism with a pluralism which recognizes the infinite possibility of relations between beings: "For the Heideggerian hegemony of Being (être) over beings (étant), we substitute as primordial the relationship between beings (étants)."[12] He is clearly advocating a move from monism to pluralism.

Furthermore, for Levinas Heidegger and Western ontology are even idolatrous. He sees Nazism as an expression of this: in the Nazi's mystified reverence for the Fatherland may be seen the worship of matter, of God pushed back into nature. For the Jew, however, God has entered history; He is in relation with man in the ethical exigency for justice, not with the ground which man inhabits:

> Mosaic revelation is the emergence of the Word before the Ego who, having questioned his origin, enters into relation with the Face. This Word detaches man from the land and sends him off in search of that other land, the promised land of the Other. This is the Word uttered by Moses and the prophets to the people of Israel, bidding them to flee Egypt and to search for Utopia. It is the Word which transforms a nation of planters into a nation of nomads. The poetic word of Parmenides is a eulogy of the past. The prophetic word of Moses differs from the poetic word of Parmenides, for whereas the former detaches us from the earth the latter attaches us to it.[13]

This attachment to the earth, to place, spells possession; the prophetic word spells trust in the paternal promise of God. Heidegger, "while denouncing the sovereignty of the technological powers of man, exalts the pre-technological powers of possession."[14] Levinas denounces this folk cult of the soil, so prevalent in Heidegger, as being a return to the pagan idolatry which Moses and the prophets sought to destroy. That sanctification of the place was concomitant with a forgetfulness of the face:

> I think of a prestigious current of modern thought issuing from Germany which inundates the pagan recesses of our Western soul. I think of Heidegger and the Heideggerians. They want man to discover the world again, which means opening oneself to the light of huge land-

scapes, to the majestic encampment of the mountains, which means returning to an infantilism mysteriously bound to place – the presence of the hearth, the opaque light of forests, the mystery of things, a jug, a pair of battered peasant shoes, the flash of a wine carafe placed on a white table cloth. Being would reveal itself behind these privileged experiences, making man its guardian. And man, the guardian of Being (that anti-human splendour), would draw from this grace his existence and truth. This indeed is the eternal seduction of paganism...[15]

What to make of this? Levinas attacks Heidegger, and yet we find innumerable influences of the latter on him. In Heidegger too we have a vital relation to otherness, though the human person and self-consciousness are not at the centre, the assessors of existence. The relation to otherness is not a Cartesian and positivist rationalism, one of "grouping" and pragmatic use; it is a relation of extreme listening "to the voice of Being"; it is a relation of extreme responsibility. For Levinas, truth is also revealed in otherness, but he develops the notion of infinity; Heidegger, that of Being. Levinas objects that Heidegger subordinates the relation with the Other to the relation with Being in general: even if this opposes the technological dominance arising from the forgetting of Being, it is nonetheless a relation of obedience to the impersonal, and leads eventually to imperialist domination and tyranny.

Yet it would be unjustified to say that Heidegger is unconcerned for the Other. In Heidegger Being is a "Mitsein," and there is a carrying of responsibility of the one for the Other. Heidegger speaks of "Fürsorge" and "Vorausspringen": We are not all nomads, each living in his own existence. Other persons do not merely constitute a multiplicity of individual subjects that appear in the world as "Personendinge" to whom we have to form some kind of relationship. No, even Robinson Crusoe could feel integrated into this world.

One must therefore ask if Levinas's critique of Heidegger is not a little exaggerated. Is he not tarring everything with the same brush, Heidegger and Western thinking? We might also ask whether Heidegger's philosophy can be called a philosophy of totality: is the priority of Being over existents equal to totality over existents? And what does Levinas intend with totality – the totality of all existents? If so, where is the problem? Totality in Levinas has a wide and varied meaning, applied to history, to the self, to political systems, to ideologies. But does conglomeration into totalities necessarily imply oppression and violation? Is this Heidegger's intent?

For Heidegger, totality, the totality of Being, is obviously not a concentration camp for all Beings, a cement enclosure into which all Beings are packed. It is the dynamic "Grund" upon which all beings happen, the dynamic conception of Being upon which new levels of beings arise and disappear, the "ens tamquam verum."

The last and most crucial point for Levinas is that of the healthier point of departure for philosophy – to face "Being" or one's fellow man. But may we not do both at the same time?

Notes:
1. Edith Wyschogrod, *Emmanuel Levinas: The Problem of Ethical Metaphysics*, (The Hague: Martinus Nijhoff, 1974), 141.
2. QLT 56.
3. DEHH 74.
4. DEHH 79.
5. DEHH 80.
6. DEHH 95.
7. DEHH 80.
8. Richard Kearney, "Emmanuel Levinas: On the Revelation of the Other" (Master's thesis, McGill University, 1977), 6-17ff.
9. Ibid.
10. DL 324.
11. Adriaan Peperzak, "Beyond Being," *Research in Phenomenology* 8 (1978): 241.
12. DL 325.
13. Kearney, 32.
14. TI 17.
15. DL 324.

9
The Other in Judaism:
Reading Levinas Between the Lines

Emmanuel Levinas, like some of his Jewish contemporaries, is an ethicist attempting to translate Old Testament transcendence into philosophical immanence. Levinas has said, "I want to translate the Bible into Greek," in which context, Greek refers to the language of the philosophers.

Why go to all the trouble? Levinas believes that we have no other option but to employ the language and concepts of Greek philosophy, because our way of reasoning is so deeply imbedded in the rationality of the Greek language. Even though Western thought has origins equally deep in a non-Greek tradition — the Judaeo-Christian culture — it has remained entirely Greek in its ways of expression.

Levinas explains:

> For me the essential characteristic of philosophy is a certain, specifically Greek, way of thinking and speaking. Philosophy is primarily a question of language; and it is by identifying the subtextual language of particular discourses that we can decide whether they are philosophical or not. Philosophy employs a series of terms or concepts — such as *morphé* (form), *ousia* (substance), *nous* (reason), *logos* (thought), or *telos* (goal), etc. — that constitute a specifically Greek lexicon of intelligibility. French and German, and indeed all of Western philosophy, is entirely shot through with this specific language; it is a token of the genius of Greek to have been able to deposit its language in the basket of Europe.[1]

Greek seems to be the only language which the philosophers can understand or even take the time to listen to. To go before a colloqium of philosophers and speak a directly religious language accentuated with biblical images taken from the prophets would be as much of a scandal today as it was for St. Paul before the *areopagite*. Nevertheless, if we speak of ethics, we cannot be fully satisfied with Greek and its purely rational concepts. A happier medium has to be found.

Although Levinas refrains from using explicitly religious language in his philosophical works, the religious perspective can still be read between the lines:

> The intrusion of the eschatological dimension into history consigned to the upsurge of the Other in *Totality and Infinity* can be seen in the perspective of traditional rabbinic commentary. Likewise, Levinas derives his emphasis upon the unique relation with the Other not only as the most immediately given datum of experience, but as a datum which is ethical in its very upsurge.[2]

Levinas does not consider himself to be a theologian. When he writes about the existence of God, it is evident that he is attempting to treat the question as a problem for Husserlian phenomenology rather than for theological explanation. Just as for Martin Buber, "Faith is not being busy with God, but rather looking for meaning in the world" (*Ich und Du*), so too for Levinas, the supernatural is not the main concern. The emphasis in Judaism is on moral interiority; and the relation with the divine is determined by the extent to which it is ethical. Thus the goal of Jewish thought is to bring to light ethical life as it is understood in traditional Jewish texts. "It is the task of the thinker to bring into the clarity of philosophical reflection the ethical insights found in the teachings of the Talmud and in the paradigmatic activities of the rabbis."[3]

In an essay entitled "Une religion d'adultes," Levinas writes:

> Moses and the prophets are not worried about the immortality of the soul but about the poor, the widow, the orphan, and the stranger. The relation with man wherein contact with the divine is accomplished is not, a sort of 'spiritual friendliness,' but is rather a test and is accomplished in an economy of justice in which every man is fully responsible. A Roman asks Rabbi Aquiba, "If your God is the God of the poor why doesn't he feed them?" "So that we may be able to escape damnation," replies Rabbi Aquiba. No one can insist more strongly on the impossibility of the situation wherein God would be the one to assume the duties and responsibilities of man.[4]

In addition, Levinas comes from Lithuania. Gershom Scholem has said of Levinas: "He's more of a Litvak than he thinks." The renowned rabbinical school in Vilnius of the eighteenth and nineteenth centuries was known for its intellectualism. In Lithuania, a sober, demystified, intellectually founded Judaism was taught which produced many rabbinical scholars, and some very capable philosophers such as Solomon Maimon. It was a secularized Judaism, and Lithuanian Jews were very proud of having held out against the assaults of the Hasidic mystical movement which was very strong in central and Eastern Europe.

In *Difficile liberté*, a collection of essays on Judaism, Levinas examines Judaism, its historical role and its essence, from different perspectives. Contemporary life does not promise wisdom, which for Levinas is the conquest of eternity, since it fails to depart from the world of events. It inaugurates no dialogue with God as did Platonic speculation. The real world no longer presents itself in its primordiality but appears transformed by man everywhere. Things are now rendered intelligible by the human imprint which they bear. Man is dominated by his world, enmeshed in a historical role, often without being able to step aside and form an objective opinion about it. The great vocation of reason is the appeal of a universal society, homogeneous in essence.

Although this situation may seem contrary to Jewish values, in many ways Jewish values parallel contemporary values. Levinas asks: "Has it not been the historical role of Judaism to de-mythologize the pagan religions of the ancient world as the modern world has been de-mythologized by science? And is not the notion of a universal society the consequence of prophetic vision?"[5]

Nevertheless, the main message that Judaism brings to the modern world arises not out of its de-mythologizing tendency, nor out of its vision of a universal society, but out of its emphasis on inner life. Contemporary man is suspicious of the life of inwardness. Through sociology, psychoanalysis, and other methods, he questions the values of inner life, trying to explain them away by referring to their conditions of social origin. According to the modern position, ideas are born and die in the societies in which they appear. Prophecy is viewed as the consequence of historical forces, as having no inner life except what is lent to it by the socio-economic forces which are eventually responsible for it. Consequently, in this current of contemporary life, Levinas sees the meaning of Israel and Judaism as having been "carried down stream." Hegelian philosophy surfaces as the biggest threat to the absolute values which the Jewish ethic is obliged to preserve:

> Therefore, Judaism for Levinas must once again serve as a corrective to trends in contemporary life. It must rediscover the interiority of the individual. Levinas claims that even Hegelian philosophy requires the disengagement of the thinker who evaluates the work of history. The historical process cannot be involved to explain away the thinker himself, because he is the one before whom the process in all its richness unfolds. To put the problem in Levinas's terms, someone must be as old as the world to think it. The contemporary world needs this point of fixity, a point of reference in the person rather than in the thought of the thinker. Having disengaged the thinker from the content of his thoughts, Levinas regards the person as the instantiation of justice, a motionless point in the world from which all truth emanates and to which all truth refers, a foundation of fixity antecedent to any thought which we can have of it or any system into which we can integrate it. Judaism is in its essence a reinstatement of the person as the final source of all values.[6]

Judaism teaches a vigorous obedience to the law that breaks the sequentiality of the historical cause and effect mode of reasoning by judging it. The contemporary world view represents an attempt to conform to its own time. If we recall chapter four on "The Trace," we remember that Levinas refers to the Trace as belonging to an immemorial past which can never be made present, neither through recollection nor effort. The trace is an anachronism. Judaism is also an anachronism in contemporary life, and it must remain so, always non-coincident with its time. Judaism maintains the temporality of interiority against the time of history. To be human, to be a responsible self, is to be an anachronism: "Monotheism and its moral revelation constitute the concrete fulfillment beyond all mythology, of the primordial anachronism of the human."[7]

The self cannot be institutionalized. Prophecy, from the standpoint of its own self-understanding, cannot be integrated into social institutions. Only the false prophet is a member of officialdom. The true prophet is totally self-sufficient. Levinas emphasizes this by offering the biblical description of Elijah whose self-sufficiency is so complete that he is outside of all economy: he is fed by ravens.

> The point of Levinas's analysis is this: history has provided no new categories for the judgement of man. What is revelatory in revelation is the modus operandi of judgement which no new data in the historical order can unseat. The Talmud "means" in the sense that it provides all categories necessary for the judgement of novelty. Everything which is required for the moral evaluation of events already pre-exists in the sacred texts. In his terms, wisdom is anterior to science and history.[8]

Levinas should not be interpreted as a naïve fundamentalist: although the Bible and its traditional commentaries provide the basis and norms for ethical judgement, he does not deny the importance or quality of historical change. Levinas has the view that man, wherever he has arisen, is fully human; that Adam does not await completion through historical process; that Israel is an ethical rather than a soteriological community. Still, he does not reject the dimension of the unanticipated, genuinely novel elements in history: "History is not an eternity simply diminished and corrupted nor the moving image of a motionless eternity; history and becoming have a positive meaning, an unpredictable fecundity, the future instant is absolutely new, but it requires history and time for its appearance."[9] In a very definite sense, Levinas's religious attitude is a contestation of the institution of Greek philosophy. What is peculiar to revelation is that it is an authentic reversal of the "natural" order of knowledge. The receiving of the Torah is an incomparable event wherein one "accepts" before "knowing." "For me, philosophy is derived from religion," says Levinas.

Levinas's reflections on Judaism as an ethical community and his fervent insistence upon ethics throughout all of his writings demonstrate how great an influence rabbinical teaching has had on him. The renowned twentieth century rabbi-philosopher, Joseph B. Soloveitchik, has also written about the indivisibility of faith and morality in Judaism,[10] saying that serving God through ethics is a Jewish concept and that it is moral schizophrenia to separate ethics from God. Furthermore, studying and acquiring knowledge is never an independent act; it always involves a sharing of divine knowledge: "In this experience, there is a merging of the finite with the infinite…" However, the acquiring of knowledge is secondary; it is first and foremost through the study of the moral order, the Torah, that man appreciates God: "through ethical preparation, intuition, not intellectual knowledge or conceptual thinking, man renders himself fit for emotional communion with the Deity."[12] The man of faith walks not behind knowledge but in front of it;

knowledge and reason are not priorities lying in his path. They can describe his faith only after the fact.

The indivisibility of ethics and faith is really a Jewish concept. It is completely contrary to the current of Christian existentialist thought as represented by Soren Kierkegaard, Fyodor Dostoyevsky, and Lev Shestov, all of whom developed their ideas independently, but saw faith as something in itself beyond all categories of reason or ethics. For Kierkegaard, faith is not an ethical life: it goes even further. Faith is belief in the power of the Absurd which can even demand a suspension of the ethical — as in the case of Abraham being called to sacrifice his son Isaac. Abraham raised his knife over Isaac and was willing to do the unethical, to become a child murderer. God stopped Abraham, at the last minute, but the fact remains that He called upon Abraham to suspend the ethical, to commit a horrid act, and this as a test of the latter's faith. This story has always troubled the rabbis. They claim that God all along never had any intention of letting Abraham sacrifice Isaac. An unethical act was never really intended and never committed. According to Kierkegaard, God stopped Abraham at the last minute not because Abraham upheld the ethical, since he was obviously ready to suspend it, but because he believed in the Absurd, and was ready to give himself over to it.

Dostoyevsky began his literary career on a very humanitarian tone with words such as these: "It deeply moves your heart to realize that the most down-trodden man, the lowest of the low, is also a human being, and is called your brother." He was concerned about the oppressed, about injustice, and was eager to change the world. About half-way through his career, his tone changed radically with *Notes From The Underground*: "I say that the world can go to pot, as long as I always get my tea." Dostoyevsky had become aware of his inability to change the world, and even conscious of the potential danger of thinking otherwise: "Moreover I maintain that an awareness of one's utter inability to help or to be of the slightest benefit or relief to suffering mankind, while simultaneously being thoroughly convinced that mankind does suffer, can even turn the love in one's heart into hatred for it."[13]

For Dostoyevsky, salvation depends upon God's mercy, independent of the actions of one's life. There is a scene in *Crime And Punishment* in which Sonia Marmeladova's father, a drunkard and a decadent man, tells how there there is a place in heaven even for people such as himself. On the day of judgement, he explains, there will be a line-up at the gates of heaven. At the front of the line will be the patriarchs, followed by the bishops, then the monks, the nuns, and the pious laity. At the end of the line will be the despicable people such as himself. When his turn finally comes to enter through the gates, St. Peter will ask him what he is doing there, waiting to get into heaven. He will implore God's mercy and St. Peter will throw up his hands in a sort of benign disgust and say, "Okay, go ahead."

Faith for Shestov, is another dimension of thought, radically different from ordinary reason and logic. Faith in God means the belief that all things are possible, as in Matthew (19:26): "For man it is impossible, but for God all things are possible." In the divine plan the laws of logic and reason, the certainties of science, lose their binding power and their meaning. Nothing is impossible for God. Thus God can demand the impossible of us, even that which surpasses all categories of reasoning and logic — of which the ethical is only a derivative. For Shestov, God is "beyond good and evil": God is not contained within moral and ethical categories. Neither can God be equated with the idea of the good.

Shestov, commenting upon Kierkegaard's interpretation of the story of Abraham, adds that Abraham believed not only in the Absurd, but also in the omnipotence of God: "God can do anything"; God can give me another son; God can do the impossible; He can bring Isaac back to life for me. Abraham had the unshakable belief that for God "all things are possible." It is precisely this boundless possibility that constitutes the operational meaning of the reality of the living God. Shestov believed that Kierkegaard had seen this in the story of Abraham, but that at certain crucial moments he did not explicitly say so; he "lost his nerve" and did not go far enough.

Finally, the question arises, if faith is separate from ethics, how is faith to be attained? For Kierkegaard, faith seems to be attainable through a kind of "audacity," the "leap of faith," a courageous stepping out into the unknown. This does not mean that man can attain faith on his own. It is pre-existent, something that can no more be destroyed by logical possibility than be created by it. Faith is something there, preceding all of man's reasoning and argumentation.[21] It is something man is called to respond to, and may shy away from.

For Dostoyevsky and Shestov, faith is a gift from God. Although Shestov also defines faith as "audacity," something that apparently can be produced by an affirmation of the human will, he clearly denies that man can by himself obtain faith. Both Dostoyevsky and Shestov seem to have believed that faith is purely a grace of God, mysteriously given to some and denied to others. Of course, even he to whom it is given may reject it; however, no one will ever find God unless he tears himself away from the seductions of reason. Dostoyevsky's hero in *Notes From The Underground* keeps repeating desperately, "I tell you that two and two do not make four!"

A) "Judaism and the Consciousness of Justice"

> *They are fanatics for social justice and proclaim that if the world is not just or in measure to become just, then it is better that it be destroyed; a point of view which is very erroneous but very fruitful, because like all desperate doctrines it produces heroism and a great awakening of human force.*
>
> An appraisal and the significance of the
Hebrew prophets from the preface to Renan's
The History of Israel.

The insistence upon justice, from this Judaism draws more spiritual force than from anything else and this is what is most responsible for Judaism's heroic persistence and perseverance. Justice must prevail.

In Judaism, the consciousness of justice is inseparable from consciousness as such. This point of view is already presupposed by the eleventh century commentator Rashi who asks why Genesis begins with the story of creation rather than with the commandments. It is because in order to possess the earth it is important for man to know that God has created it. This way he knows that the earth is a gift from God and not his by usurpation. He has learned that to possess is already to have received. He also has learned that every man has the right to vital living space. He sees his possession of the earth as an investiture which puts his own personal freedom into question. He cannot call the earth his own property, understood in the strict Roman sense of the term. His own consciousness of self does not reveal any rights to him. His freedom is arbitrary. The normal exercise of his "I" that transforms everything it touches into his, is put into question. The peasant will not think of the eternal connections which attach him to the earth, but will rather think of himself as a child of Aram — his ancestor who was a wanderer.

In this way consciousness of self becomes moral consciousness. The peasant who is attached to the earth without the necessity of justifying his claim to property, knows that his ancestor, a child of Aram who was a wanderer had to legitimate his right of ownership. The consciousness of self discovers itself to be illegitimate — owing to another. "To be for oneself is already to know the transgression which I've committed towards the other."[14] Therefore, "the moral self appears at the outset of Jewish tradition as its elementary mode of being. For Levinas, the ethical is not an adventitious addition to a vision of God, but belongs to it essentially."[15] As Levinas writes, "The moral relation reunites the consciousness of self and the consciousness of God at the same time. Ethics is not the corollary of the vision of God, it is the vision itself. Ethics is an optics."[16]

All morality is grounded in a heteronomous will. To know God is already obedience to another. To know God is to know what one has to do, but knowing what one has to do without being robbed of one's freedom. For Levinas, heteronomy is not the imposition of a divine will, but a revelation through the appearance of other persons. His thought is consistent with that of the traditional Jewish thinker who held that the Other does not compel but rather solicits. The Other does not impose himself as an alien will destructive to freedom. Heteronomy is thus affirmed as an absolutely passive principle of alterity which founds moral action. It is based on the Jewish understanding of the Other as the one who is suffering and helpless, who cannot compel but only solicit and appeal. To know God is to obey the will of the Other. Levinas refers to Mainmonides who said that the manner of knowing God by negative attributes takes on a positive expression in morality. "God is merciful," means "be merciful like Him."

In the face of the Other the realm of the transcendent is opened:

> In an ethical relation, the Other presents himself as absolutely Other, but this radical alterity in relation to myself neither destroys nor denies my freedom, as the philosophers think. The ethical relation is anterior to the opposition of freedoms, to war, which according to Hegel, inaugurates history. The face of my neighbour has an alterity which is not allegorical, it opens towards the beyond.[17]

Justice becomes the essence behind all Jewish piety. "Justice rendered to my neighbour gives me an insurmountable closeness to God,"[18] and this justice is learned in Jewish ritual practice. Obedience to the ritual law constitutes a discipline that tends towards justice. In obeying ritual law, the demand of the Other is recognized; the Other in this case, God, has a right to suppress the egoity of the Self. "The law is effort. Daily fidelity to the ritual demands a courage which is more calm, more noble and greater than that of a warrior."[19]

The way to God is by way of discipline to ritual. Its greatness is in its daily practice. The law is true self-education, supreme instruction. What is done is done because it is commanded and one chooses to obey the commandment. The Christian emphasis on love is not in the forefront because even love itself first demands justice. Levinas emphasizes the importance of Jewish ritual practice with the following passage:

> Here is a passage where three opinions are enunciated: The second indicates the way in which the first is true and the third indicates the practical conditions of the second. Ben Zomma said, 'I found a verse which contains the entire Torah: Hear O Israel the Lord our God is One.' Ben Nanas said, 'I found a verse which contains the entire Torah: Love thy neighbour as thyself.' Ben Pazi said, 'I found a verse which contains the entire Torah: Thou shalt sacrifice one lamb in the morning and the other in the evening.' And Rabbi, their teacher, stood up and decided: 'The law is according to Ben Pazi.'[20]

In addition to the centrality of ritual there is also a distinct messianism, a sense of mission in the Judaism of Levinas. One is born a Jew and this identity is anterior to all other goals in life:

> The Jew is responsible for all of creation; Jewish identity is 'patience, fatigue and responsibility.' It is the very opposite of Western world views which refuse obedience without an a priori act of acquiescence so that personal sovereignty is always maintained. The spontaneous acceptance of Jewish life is replaced in Western thought by a distancing of oneself from whatever is accepted.[21]

Jewish praxis, both ritual and ethical, is prior to understanding. It is the Pharisee who struggles with questions and obtains answers not through violence but through intellectual conflict. His entering the divine realm is not always all that enthusiastic. He is there to battle in a world which, when left by God to its own devices, sacrifices man to the philosophy of their instincts. Since these are the instincts that dominate the world, it follows that those like himself who preserve the divine presence in the world will be the first to fall victim to this domination. He waits in the expectation of justice in a yet unredeemed world. Nevertheless, he searches for divine presence in the "non-incarnate word" seeing the relation between God and man not in a communion of feeling, in love, but a relation between minds, through the teaching of the Torah.

Levinas supports the theme of election in Jewish thought: being a Jew is not only an identity but also being one of the chosen. Levinas explains that the theme of election does not represent any kind of aristocratic pretension, — it symbolizes a surplus of responsibility, a surplus of obligation: "I am the one who is responsible and not another. I am unique in the sense that I have been elected to care for my neighbour and I can't pass off this election to another; responsibility is irrevocable."[22] The feeling of election obliges one to care for the Other and to respect him as Other, alien and unknowable (*étranger et inconnaissable*). In fact, the Jew is the very condition of justice in the world: in order to have a humane and just society, someone must take responsibility for others. The Jew is necessary to man because he is a hostage to all others; without him morality would not know where to begin. The Jew is a new kind of man. He has been elected not by virtue of his race but by virtue of the law which he has received. He belongs to a community of judges, who by practicing the law are able to resist temptation; a community vital to the assurance of justice in the world. Election is not a religious category but an ethical one.

Levinas does not want to give the impression that the Jews have cornered the market on justice and morality. The idea behind the role of the Jew as a chosen one is that morality and justice must have their foundation within man and not within institutions, that often do a very poor job of protecting them. What Levinas wants to say is that the Jew, having been subjected to a very long history of injustice and inhumanity is perhaps more able than anyone else to understand the necessity of finding moral certitude within oneself. Given his personal experience with long term injustice, the Jew has an important contribution to make to the world, one that all men can learn and benefit from.

Even when the true source of morality is within the individual, institutions are still needed in order to ensure that a society will function more or less harmoniously. This, says Levinas, is where the 'Greeks' see their duty to perform. When it comes to politics, questions of state, systems of justice, courts or proceedings, it is time for Greek wisdom, Greek political thought and Greek logic.

Normally, states are founded with "a little bit of reason and a little bit of Greek spirit." However, the point of departure is the supposition that men are wolves against wolves: a state is needed to have order. But why not have a state based on the notion that man is responsible for his fellow man? This is the message of Judaism, the one that Levinas is forever seeking to translate into 'Greek,' that politicians and philosophers too might come to understand and apply its wisdom.

B) "Judaism and History"

Levinas offers us Judaism as a standard in an inaccessible past, outside of history, and yet he allows for the unpredictable in history, for becoming: 'History and becoming have a positive meaning.' Is this not a contradiction? How are the two reconcilable?

Once again the problem comes down to Levinas's enthusiasm as a 'visionary,' which often leaves a detailed explanation wanting. There is history and there is history; there is history and there is us. There is the history of totality in which the subject is lost in the logos of reason, and from which Levinas encourages us to escape, and there is the history from which the philosopher cannot escape: the history of departures from totality; history as the very moment of transcendence, of the excess over the totality, without which no totality would appear as such.

Judaism offers such a possibility. Judaism gives man a standard of perfection that is radically other and transcendent. For Franz Rosenzweig, the Synagogue is an oasis of this radically different standard where the thirsty soul can go for replenishment. In *The Star of Redemption* Rosenzweig writes, "it is only in the Synagogue, uninvolved in history and its injustices, stubbornly living its inner and separate life which we can see with the prophetic eye of inner vision the last and most distant things. The Synagogue already knows the eschaton."[23]

By way of Judaism we acquire a sort of "trans-historical condition through which the subject is no longer lost in the logos of reason and history, but remains capable of directing and judging history from the vantage point of an orientating meaning."[24] History loses its totalizing character and acquires a new dynamism:

> The Other's face is an ethical appeal inviting us to modify ever anew the meaning of history in the light of an absolute meaning and of a radically different future: the future of the Other. While Heidegger experiences the future as the way in which the alternating finite periods of world history befall us, Levinas experiences it first as the coming of the Other (*la visitation*), as it concretely takes shape, for instance in the birth of the child. In this way history receives an absolute and infinite future and turns into salvation history.[25]

In practical terms, what this means is that we stop judging man by his works. It means that we must learn that the judgement of history is pronounced by survivors on the works of the dead, who are no longer around to explain their deeds or defend them. It means that we shall see that judgement is often crude and subjective varying from place to place and from time to time. We do not accept this judgement as final but seek to separate ourselves from this course of history in order to make judgements of our own with reference to "a standard of perfection that is radically Other and transcendent."[26] "History" itself is therefore not the final judge of history.

What Levinas wishes to describe is a subject who stands in the totality while being radically withdrawn from it. The foundation of this withdrawal is situated in the ethical relation, as given to us in Judaism. This relation breaks through the totality and develops a meaning which can no longer be confined within the immanent order of things. Similarly, the Idea of the Infinite does not take shape in thought and reason, but in the ethical relation that 'breaks through.' For Levinas, "thinking and the occurrence of truth remain thoroughly historical, while in the ethical dimension they acquire at the same time a trans-historical dimension. . ."[27]

This does not mean that history as it is generally understood is meaningless — quite the contrary: in light of the trans-historical Judaic dimension we have all the more reason to try and make the world a better place. The very nature of Judaism calls for this. Levinas presents Judaism as having a horizontal relation to the divine; in Christianity the relation is vertical and, according to Jewish thinking, places an over-emphasis on personal salvation, and has a profound pessimism concerning human history. He explains that in Heidegger this verticality has manifested itself in ontological rootedness; in Christianity, in the parable of the two kingdoms. Judaism, however, negates this pessimism, affirming the essential nature of man's ethical relation with man in history. Avoiding all extremes of verticality, it sees history not as a hopeless reality to be escaped, but as a means to human justice.

Herman Cohen, in *Religion of Reason out of the Sources of Judaism*, goes even further, saying Judaism is by its very nature political: in it faith and ethical practice go hand in hand. He says that the Hebrew word for righteousness (*tsédek*) is the same word for piety in general. The real spiritual focus of Jewish creativity is prophecy, and the distinguishing characteristic of the prophetic idea is 'the notion that religion and politics are inseparable.'

To conclude, it is evident that the greatest influence of Jewish teaching on Levinas is in the primacy given to the Other. Aside of its ritual aspects, the entire Bible is an ethics of behaviour with respect to the Other through all degrees and levels. It is too much an integral source of Western culture to be ignored in philosophy.

Notes:
[1] "Dialogue with Emmanuel Levinas" interview by Richard Kearney, in: *Face to Face with Levinas*, ed. Richard Cohen (Albany: State University of New York Press, 1986), 19.
[2] Edith Wyschogrod, *Emmanuel Levinas: The Problem of Ethical Metaphysics*, (The Hague: Matinus Nijhoff, 1974.), 159.
[3] Ibid., 60.
[4] DL 36.
[5] DL 233.
[6] Wyschogrod,162.
[7] DL 237
[8] Wyschogrod,163.
[9] DL 173.
[10] See; Rabbi Abraham R. Besidin, *Reflections of the Rav: Lessons in Jewish Thought adapted from the teachings of Rabbi Joseph B. Soloveitchik* (Jerusalem: Alpha Press, 1979).
[11] Ibid., 71.
[12] Ibid.

[13] Quoted in Lev Shestov, *Dostoyevsky, Tolstoy and Nietzsche*, trans. Bernard Martin and Spencer Roberts (Athens Ohio: Ohio University Press, 1968), 222.
[14] DL 33.
[15] Wyschogrod, 164.
[16] DL 33.
[17] DL 34.
[18] DL 34.
[19] DL 35.
[20] DL 166
[21] Wyschogrod, 167.
[22] François Poirie, *Emmanuel Lévinas: Qui êtes-vous?* (Lyon: La Manufacture, 1987) 116.
[23] Franz Rosenzweig, *The Star of Redemption*, trans. William W. Hallo (New York: Holt & Winston, 1971).
[24] Luk Bouckaert, "Ontology and Ethics: Reflections on Levinas's Critique of Heidegger," *International Philosophical Quarterly 10* (1970): 415.
[25] Ibid.
[26] John Wild, "Introduction" in TI.
[27] Bouckaert, 415.

10
Ethics and Judaism, or the Numinous

A) Judaism and the Numinous

With so much emphasis on Judaism as an ethical community, how is the holiness of God to be understood?

According to Levinas, the rabbis understood divine holiness in a way which undermines its significance as numinosity. Judaism has disenchanted the world (*le judaisme a désensorcelé le monde*).[1] The numinous carries man beyond his own powers, but in a kind of divine transport which is an offense to human freedom. The uncontrollable seizure which constitutes the human experience of the numinous eliminates the relation between persons, the foundation of all ethics. The numinous, by means of ecstasy, makes men participate in a drama they have not chosen and eventually leads to their ruin. It strikes at human freedom, which, though not an end in itself, is still the presupposition without which human values cannot be realized: "The holy which engulfs me and transports me is violence."[2] The God of Israel is not a survivor who comes along after the departure of mythical pagan deities; He is radically different from them. Jewish monotheism, says Levinas, is a break with a specific concept of the holy. It does not consolidate the cosmic powers so that its God represents the sum of all power; it does not arrange the pagan manifestations of the numinous into hierarchies; rather it denies them. Before these pagan conceptions of the holy, Judaism is atheism, "a-theos," a god-lessness: a de-idolized, de-mythologized religiosity.

Judaism is understood as a separation, a radical severance. The spirituality of Israel is lived as an atheism which has freed itself from the numinality of primitive religion and emerged as a free self. Judaism appears when knowledge and truth have become possible; it represents an access to truth without ecstatic experience. It presupposes human sovereignty and the value of consciousness. Consciousness appropriates reality without engulfing it: "To be 'conscious of' is the very opposite of possession in the sense that consciousness does not touch the independence of the existent to which it addresses itself. It resists the violence of enthusiasm and the absorption by a reality outside the self which obliterates the distinction between self and world."[3] In this sense, Levinas maintains, Judaism understands itself as being very close to Western philosophy:

> It is not by simple coincidence that the way of synthesis between Jewish revelation and Greek thought was masterfully traced out by Maimonides ... that the wise men of the Talmud already had a deep respect for Greek wisdom; that for the Jew, education and instruction go hand in hand; and that an ignoramus does not know how to be really pious. These curious Talmudic texts which attempt to present the nature of the spirituality of Israel as residing in its intellectual excellence are quite frequent. It is not a luciferious pride of reason, but it is because intellectual excellence is interior ... and most of all because it does not destroy the conditions of action and effort. Of course, in Jewish religious life the importance of the exercise of the intellect is always first applied to the content of revelation, to the Torah.[4]

Levinas says that Judaism's rejection of the numinous is not a return to a religious rationalism in a dogmatic, Kantian sense. On the contrary, all of twentieth century theology, Jewish and Christian, has been marked by a renewed quest for "the living God," as opposed to the Aristotelian and scholastic "God of the philosophers." Levinas takes part in this renewed quest: "God can only be understood in terms of the interhuman perspective... God must be thought in the ethical perspective, and not in the ontological perspective of our being there or of some supreme being and creator correlative to the world, as traditional metaphysics often held."[5]

For Levinas, God reveals himself discretely as a Trace, not an ontological presence, a self-thinking thought, as for Aristotle; neither is God, as in scholastic metaphysics, an *Ipsum Esse Subsistens* or an *Ens Causa Sui*. Levinas bases his faith on the God of the Bible, who cannot be defined or proved by means of logical predictions and attributions. Even the superlatives of wisdom, power and causality are inadequate before the absolute otherness of God. All we can do is look for the "Trace of God" as revealed in particular interhuman events that open towards transcendence. That is why for Levinas God is to be found in ethics, and is not an overbearing almighty numinous force.

Yet the numinous and ethics are not necessarily contradictory. The word numinous, popularized in Rudolf Otto's classic work on the philosophy of religion, *The Idea of the Holy*, has become the cornerstone for many theologies of "the living God." Levinas's use of the word 'numinous', though by way of refutation, seems to be a play on Otto's *The Idea of the Holy*. Levinas does not refer directly to the aforementioned work, but there can be no doubt that he has it in mind. Rudolf Otto begins his book with a quotation from Goethe: "Das Schaudern ist der Menschheit bestes Teil. Wie auch die Welt ihm das Gefühl verteuere, ergriffen fühlt er tief das ungeheuere." (To shudder is humanity's best part. No matter how much the world impedes this feeling, deep down inside it feels the tremendous). Levinas begins one of his essays with the first part of this quotation: "Das Schaudern ist der menschheit bestes Teil." He omits the second half because Judaism has already progressed beyond a God who is a "mysterium tremens," to a God of justice. Rudolf Otto would not deny this; every developed religion has already effectuated "a break with a specific concept of the sacred." Yet the experience of the numinous still remains the basic underlying element of all religious experience — even for Judaism.

B) Kant and Schleiermacher

The move away from the God of Aristotle, a medieval concept of God, towards a God found in ethics, was initiated by Kant. But Kant was still far from developing any theology of a living God.

In the *Critique of Pure Reason* Kant treats the "problem of God" in traditional rationalistic metaphysics. "There are only three ways of proving the existence of God by means of speculative reason."[6]: the ontological, the cosmological, and the physical-theological. All three are subjected to an analysis — for Kant, the *sine qua non* for arriving at "knowledge" of God — and found to be inconsequential (*unschlüssig*). Though Kant could not prove the existence of God by speculative reason, Kant saw that reason is no more able to establish a contrary position, and he therefore turns to a moral proof for the existence of God. This he begins with the statement: "I had to suspend knowledge in order to leave some room for faith."[7] Although there exist various versions of the moral proof for the existence of God, the most effective is "the existence of God as a postulate of pure practical reason."⁸ The incentive for this proof is the concept of the "highest good," in which morality and happiness are united and which is at the same time the object of moral law. Kant says that as well as our knowledge of objects, which is originally given in sense intuition, there is moral knowledge, an *a priori* knowledge of what men ought to do — i.e., to promote the highest good. Men ought not to tell lies; this we know whether we lie or not: this knowledge is obligatory. But where does this sense of moral obligation come from? Kant believes that to find a cause one must postulate the existence of God. The essence of the Kantian "proof" for the existence of God is contained in the sentence, "It is the highest good (which must be possible) that we should try to promote."⁹

The "proof" above is founded on the meaning of human existence, on the meaning of reality. Reality harmonizes with morality, and vice versa: it is not immoral, not indifferent to morality. In his *Critique of Judgement*, Kant develops this thought from a teleological context: moral teleology, the tendency in nature towards the realization of the highest good, leads to moral theology. Kant's argument begins with practical reason and leads to a "faith of reason" (*Vernunftglauben*), a knowledge of God arising out of a need (*Bedurfnis*) of pure practical reason, "a knowledge of God, but only in a practical relation."¹⁰

By way of practical reason, the transcendental ideals "are assertorically defined as those which correspond to real objects"¹¹; by such means a practically founded metaphysics is established. Nevertheless the reality of these metaphysical ideas remains a problem for speculative reason.

The fact that the meaning of life is closely related to morality prepares the way for religion: "The moral law leads by way of the concept of the highest good... to religion, i.e. to the knowledge of all obligations as divine commands."¹² Thus the concept of God belongs to morality. Kant proceeds to apply his principles of moral religion to Christianity: what is communicated in the Bible through revelation can also be attained by reason. Kant understands Christian dogma as being symbolical presentations of natural "truths" — that is why he often distinguishes between a "historical-ecclesiastical" faith (*Geschichtsglauben-Kirchenglauben*) and a faith of "reason" (*Vernunftglauben*).

In Kantian moral religion, man is the measure of all things, of the supernatural as well as the historical, and everything is in the service of moral perfection. The most genuine religion is the religion of a moral life.

The truths of revelation are not denied, but rather employed in the service of religion as moral consciousness. Kant was against all ritual in religion. True ritual, true religious service is a "service of the heart ... and can only exist in the reflection upon and upholding of, all obligations as divine commands." Jesus is represented as the idea of humanity as a moral essence, the community of the church is converted into an "ethical community" having as its task the convergence of all humanity into a "Republic of the Laws of Virtue" (*Republik der Tugendgesetze*). God, Kant says, "is not an essence outside of me ... God is the moral-practical reason."[13]

In modern times, the move away from a purely rational concept of God was initiated by Friedrich Schleiermacher. Schleiermacher opted for a renewed understanding of religion, one neither dogmatic nor rationalistic, but based upon personal experience. Schleiermancher is very original for the period in which he lived and wrote — the heyday of German idealism. Everyone was concerned about the Absolute, the relation between the infinite and the finite, and the life of the Spirit. The three great German idealists — Fichte, Hegel, and Schelling — viewed religion as an expression of the finite spirit's relation to the divine reality. All three were constructors of philosophical systems, and naturally tried to interpret religion through the principles of their systems. But was this religion? As Otto wrote in his introduction to Schleiermacher's book *On Religion*,"One was cultured and full of ideals; one was aesthetic, and one was moral. But one was no longer religious."[14] Fichte tended to reduce religion to ethics; Hegel to depict it as a form of knowledge; and Schelling to interpret the development of the religious consciousness as that of a higher knowledge. Schleiermacher approached religion from a different point of view — that of a preacher and theologian who distinguishes religious consciousness from metaphysics and ethics: "In order to make quite clear to you what is the original and characteristic possession of religion, it resigns, at once, all claims on anything that belongs either to science or morality."[15]

For Schleiermacher the "religious experience" or "religious feeling" was essentially an intuition, a "feeling of dependence." Using the idealist language of his era, Schleiemacher arrives at this feeling of dependence thus: Thought can conform itself to being, as with scientific or theoretical knowledge; the being corresponding to the totality of our scientific concepts and judgements is what is called Nature. Thought can also cause being to conform. In moral activity, which has thinking as its basis, the moral agent seeks to make being conform to thought; the totality expressing itself in thought-directed action is called Spirit.

There is an apparent dualism here: on the one hand, Nature-being-object; on the other, Spirit-thought-subject. These are united, each coming into identity with the other in the universe or God. This identity cannot be comprehended by conceptual thought, but only felt. The feeling is linked to self-consciousness — not a reflective self-awareness, apprehending the identity in the diversity of its moments or phrases, but an immediate self-consciousness, equaling feeling. At this fundamental level, immediate feeling, the distinctions and oppositions of conceptual thought have not emerged. We can speak of it as an intuition, but it is not a clear intellectual intuition:

> That is to say, the self does not enjoy any intellectual intuition of the divine totality as direct and sole object; but it feels itself as dependent on the totality which transcends all oppositions."[16] "This feeling of dependence (*Abhängigkeitsgefühl*) is the 'religious side' of self-consciousness: it is in fact the 'religious feeling.' For the essence of religion is neither thought nor action, but intuition and feeling. It seeks to intuit the universe ... And the universe, as Schleiermacher uses the term, is the infinite divine reality. Hence religion is for him essentially or fundamentally the feeling of dependence upon the infinite.[17]

Religion then, for Schleiermacher, is not metaphysical deduction, knowledge, or morality, but feeling. In his book *On Religion*, Schleiermacher admonishes his readers to "wake up" to this, for once to examine their feelings. Otto parallels Schleiermacher: the religious experience for him is not the product of pure rationalism, metaphysical speculation, ethics, and morals, but has a non-rational basis. In Otto this is the numinous; in Schleiermacher the feeling of dependence. Schleiermacher turns his back on the reduction by Kant and Fichte of religion to morals. He rejects any attempt to exhibit the essence of religion as a form of theoretical knowledge: "Wherefore, my friends, belief must be something different from a mixture of opinions about God and the world, and of precepts for one life or for two. Piety cannot be an instinct craving for a mess of metaphysical and ethical crumbs."[18]

This does not mean that there is no connection at all between religion, metaphysics, and ethics. Schleiermacher posits one, one somewhat different than that posited by Rudolf Otto, as we shall see below. Otto demonstrates the necessity of the rational in religious experience; Schleiermacher maintains that it is the rational — metaphysics and ethics — which stands in need of religion. Metaphysics and ethics both need the intuition of religion in order to become concrete, in order to grasp man's dependence upon God, in order not to remain mere theories.

C) Rudolf Otto: The Idea of the Holy.

If one is to look at Otto's presentation of the "idea of the holy," a few points of translation must be made clear. Levinas makes a distinction between the "sacred" (*le sacré*) and the "holy" (*le saint*). The sacred is the elevation of natural things to the level of the divine, out of fear of the inability to rationalize them; the holy is the desire for the Infinite. The sacred gives us magic; the holy communicates to us the Transcendent. With Otto writing in German there is no such distinction: *das Heilige* can mean either the sacred or the holy. The French translation of Otto's book is called *Le Sacré*, the English, *The Idea of the Holy*. "The Idea of the Sacred" would probably have been a more accurate title for the latter, as the word "holy" implies "holiness," moral virtuousness, which does not enter into Otto's analysis. Otto is dealing not with Judaism, which equates religion with morality, but religious experience. Yet as *das Heilige* is regularly translated as "the holy" in the English translation from which all quotes in the following account are taken, no change has been made. The reader, however, might do well to read "the sacred" in these instances.

Otto, like Schleiermacher, wanted to get away from the over-rationalization of religion; beyond its objectivity, beyond church teachings and dogma, beyond morality, rites and institutions; to get to the nucleus of religion and present it as something "living." This is the genius of Otto, as Mircea Eliade explains:

> Instead of studying the ideas of God and religion, Rudolf Otto set to work to analyse the modalities of religious experience. Gifted with great psychological discrimination and fortified by training, both as a theologian and a historian of religions, he succeeded in isolating the content and the specific character of that experience. Neglecting the rational and speculative aspects of religion, he concentrated especially upon its non-rational side.[19]

Otto's *The Idea of the Holy* begins by giving the reader a definition of what is rational. The rational is "an object that can thus be thought conceptually." With regard to God, especially for the Christian, the rational would mean the many concepts, attributes which the deity receives, or by which He is understood — e.g., spirit, reason, purpose, good will, supreme power, unity, selfhood. Any religion which recognizes and maintains a view of God through these concepts is a "rational religion"; it is precisely this abundance of conceptions about God which distinguishes a religion's "high rank and superior value." These conceptions also diminish the danger of a religion's becoming mere feeling, an "intoxicated frenzy."

As inspiring as rational conceptions of the deity may be, they do not by any means constitute all of religious experience. They remain the predicates of a non-rational or supra-rational subject, which they can but imply. They are essential attributes of their implied subject, but they do not present it in its entirety. As Otto elaborates:

> They are 'essential' (and not merely accidental) attributes of that subject, but they are also, it is important to notice, synthetic essential attributes. That is to say, we have to predicate them of a subject which they qualify; but which in deeper essence is not, nor indeed can be comprehended in them; which rather requires comprehension of a quite different kind.[20]

There is a deeper element behind all religious experience, which Otto describes as the non-rational, and to which he dedicates the greater part of *The Idea of the Holy*. In order to arrive at a "balanced" religious experience, one must understand this non-rational element as being in interplay with the "rational."

I) The Numinous

"The holy" once possessed a meaning very different from the one normally attributed to it today. "We generally take 'holy' as meaning 'completely good'," says Otto; "It is the absolute moral attribute, denoting the consummation of moral goodness."[21] This is so because the process of moralization and rationalization which religion has undergone in modern times, especially at the hands of philosophers such as Kant. Originally, according to Otto, "holy" bore reference only to an "overplus" — an experience of something supra-natural, an "unnamed something"; "if the ethical was present at all, it was not original, and never constituted the whole meaning of the word."[22]

This category, "the holy," is nonetheless at the heart of religion: "there is no religion in which it does not live as the real innermost core, and without it no religion would be worthy of the name."[23] Hebrew *qadôsh,* Greek *hagios,* and Latin *sanctus* do encompass the idea of absolute goodness, but only at the highest stage of their development: "This 'holy' represents the gradual shaping and filling in with ethical meaning, or what we shall call 'schematization' of what was a unique original feeling — response, which can be in itself ethically neutral, and claims consideration in its own right."[24] To indicate that which in the meaning of "holy" is above and beyond goodness, Otto adapts the Latin word *numen*, forming the category of "the numinous." He also speaks of a "numinous" state of mind, explaining that although this mental state is *sui generis* and irreducible to any other, it cannot be strictly defined.

Otto establishes this terminology in the second chapter of his book; he expands upon the numinous throughout the following eleven chapters. He begins with the numinous as a "creature feeling," and ends with the expression of the numinous in art and illustrations of the numinous in the Bible and in the writings of Martin Luther.

The numinous is first of all a creature-feeling, or "creature-consciousness" — in contrast to Schleiermacher's 'feeling of dependence.' Otto gives the example of Abraham pleading with God for the men of Sodom: "Behold now, I have taken upon me to speak unto the Lord, which am but dust and ashes" (Gen. 18:27); the numinous is "the emotion of a creature, submerged and overwhelmed by its own nothingness in contrast to that which is supreme above all creatures."[25]

II) The Numinous as the *Mysterium Tremendum.*

The numinous as the *mysterium tremendum* is best summed up by the word "awe." Otto says, "faith unto salvation, trust, love — all these are there. But over and above these is an element which may also on occasion, quite apart from them, profoundly affect us and occupy the mind with a bewildering strength."[26] This is the feeling of awe that one finds in sudden ebullitions of personal piety; during the solemnities of rites and liturgies; in the atmosphere that clings to old religious monuments and to temples and churches. Otto calls the *mysterium tremendum* the "element of awefulness," normally referred to as the "fear of God." This is no ordinary, "natural" fear but rather a "shuddering" (*grauen*); "it implies that the mysterious is already beginning to loom before the mind, to touch the feelings."[27] It is the Hebrew *hiqdish* (hallow). It is also what characterizes the so-called "religion of primitive man," appearing as a daemonic dread. It is what makes one's "blood run cold" and one's "flesh crawl"; that dread which penetrates "to the marrow." Only in the "highly-developed" religions, such as Christianity, has the "shudder" lost its crazy, bewildering dimension; yet even here there is something ineffable that holds the mind.

Into this "element of awefulness" enters the *orgé,* the "Wrath of Yahweh." The *orgé* is frequently subjected to rationalization and filled in with elements derived from moral reason — righteousness in requital and punishment for moral transgression. The *orgé* is supra-rational; it "throbs and gleams, palpable and visible, in the 'wrath of God,' prompting a sense of 'terror' that no 'natural' anger can arouse."[28]

Otto talks about the "absolute overpoweringness" of the numinous — the *majestas.* Here especially "creature consciousness" becomes evident: "Thus in contrast to the 'overpowering' of which we are conscious as an object over against the self, there is the feeling of one's own submergence, of being but 'dust and ashes' and nothingness."[29] It is the cry of Abraham: "Who am I but dust and ashes?"

Taken as a category of value, the holy refers to man's veneration of the numinous (*Tu solus sanctus*) — his own feeling of unworth is expressed by his consciousness of sin and the desire for atonement:

> It is the positive numinous value or worth, and to it corresponds on the side of the creature a numinous disvalue or 'unworth'... Nonetheless, a profoundly humble and heartfelt recognition of 'the holy' may occur in particular experience without being always or definitely charged or infused with the same sense of moral demands.[30]

This is reminiscent of a theme recurrent in the writings of Dostoyevsky: the hope of gaining salvation through degradation and suffering. The theme is profoundly expressed in *Notes from the Underground*. The lack of moral imperative separates it from the Kantian religious comprehension. The greater the discrepancy between numinous-worth and creaturely-unworth, the greater the level of religious development: "No religion has brought the mystery of the need for atonement, or expiation to so complete, so profound, or so powerful expression as Christianity."[31]

The third experience of the numinous as "mysterium tremendum" is the "element of energy or urgency." Vividly perceptible in the *orgé* or "wrath," it clothes itself in symbolical expressions — vitality, passion, emotional temper, will, force, movement, excitement, activity, impetus. These features are typical and recur again and again from the daemonic level up to the idea of the "living God."

Thus the *tremendum*. But what is the *mysterium*? It is simply the "wholly other" (*thateron, anyad, alienum*) — the mystery, different from the stupor of the *tremendum*, "the astonishment that strikes us dumb." The *mysterium* cannot be grasped nor subjected to analogy, as can the *tremendum* ; words cannot express it. Mysticism calls it "nothingness."

> Not content with contrasting it with all that is of nature, or this world, mysticism concludes by contrasting it with Being itself and all that 'is,' and finally actually calls it 'that which is nothing.' By this 'nothing' is meant not only that of which nothing can be predicated, but that which is absolutely and intrinsically other than and opposite of everything that is and can be thought.[32]

It is absence supreme. The *mysterium* and *tremendum*, taken together, form the *mysterium fascinans* — a supreme fascination "radiating the perfect plenitude of being."[33]

Otto and Levinas are in agreement on one thing — the irreducibility of the wholly Other, the totally Other; its complete elusiveness, or, in the terminology of phenomenology, its Absence. Otto seeks to avoid the reduction of his "wholly other" to a moral or ethical sphere. With Levinas it is only through ethics that we get an inkling of the Infinite. Levinas rejects outright the notions of numinosity and "absolute overpoweringness."

Otto goes on to form a synthesis between ethics and religion, one different from that of Levinas.

III) The Rational and Non-Rational in Active Interplay

We now see that in religious experience there are two processes of development taking place — the rational and the non-rational. If the rational element is impoverished, the danger of religious "intoxication" or fanaticism arises; if the non-rational numinous elements are obscured, one is left with a mere ethical teaching much in the Kantian tradition. "We must no longer understand by 'the holy' or 'sacred' the numinous in general, nor even the numinous at its highest development; we must always understand thereby the numinous completely permeated, saturated with elements signifying rationality, purpose, personality, morality."[34] Otto explains that "primitive" daemonic dread is not of rational or moral origin, but non-rational; it is an occurrence to which the mind responds in a unique way. This daemonic dread undergoes development; becomes "rationalized" and "moralized," filled with ethical meaning, as in Judaism. It rises to the level of "fear of the gods." False analogies are gradually dispelled. The numen becomes God or Deity, who is then termed holy (*sanctus, hagios*).

Subsequently, a social consciousness of rationalization and moralization based on the numinous consciousness begins to grow. This is where the ideals of justice, obligation, goodness and the "will of God" enter: "more and more, these ideals come to enter into the very essence of the numen and charge it with ethical content."[35] The holy becomes the good, the sacrosanct, then the good and sacrosanct; finally, "no God is like the God of Israel." This rationalization and moralization of the numinous, grows ever more clear and potent. "It is in fact the most essential part of what we call 'the history of salvation.' We prize it as the ever-growing self-revelation of the divine."[36]

Otto wants next to demonstrate the connection between the rational and the non-rational elements, their inward and necessary union in formal religion. He recounts religious experiences among tribal peoples as witnessed by missionaries; he elaborates upon his hypothesis that "as the rational elements come together in the historical evolution of religions with the non-rational, they serve to 'schematize' these."[37] The *tremendum,* the daunting and repelling moment of the numinous, is schematized by means of the rational ideas of justice and moral will — it becomes the holy "wrath of God"; the *fascinans*, the attracting moment of the numinous, is schematized by means of the idea of goodness, mercy, love — it becomes that which we mean by Grace; "the *mysterium* is schematized by absolute rational attributes applied to the Deity."

The reason for the correspondence of the "mysterious" and the absoluteness of rational attributes is that our understanding can only encompass the relative; "that which is in contrast absolute, though it may in a sense be thought, cannot be thought home, thought out, it is within reach of our conceiving, but it is beyond the grasp of our comprehension."³⁸ This is the only way that one is capable of talking about God. However, due to the elusiveness of the mysterious, there is a danger of completely losing "sight" of it, and falling into pure "rationalism." Therefore the constant interaction of the two elements is a necessity.

> By the rational living activity of its non-rational elements a religion is guarded from passing into "rationalism." By being steeped in, and saturated with rational elements, it is guarded from sinking into fanaticism or mere mysticality, or at least from persisting in these, and is qualified to become a religion for all civilized humanity. The degree in which both rational and non-rational elements are jointly present, united in healthy and lovely harmony, affords a criterion to measure the relative rank of religions..."³⁹

For Otto, Lutheran Christianity is the highest form of all religion, in its abundance of rational concept, and in its deep mysticism that is yet not mysticality.

Despite the popularity of his book, the international acclaim it received, and its translation into a dozen languages, Otto's central theme, that of the non-rational, the holy and the numinous, was severely criticized. Some critics found him too much in the Kantian rationalistic tradition against which he was writing. These doubtless reject any kind of "rational" speech about God, any attempt to define Him through absolute attributes, such as goodness, justice, or love. Otto saw these attributes as analogy, and considered them perfectly legitimate for the "practical purposes of talking about God"; in no way would he have reduced God to them. His main concern was to show that in religious experience there is a kind of primordial alertness, before all explication or rationalization, before all dogma or moral teaching. This primordial alertness is at the core of religion, Judaism included.

This lengthy detour into the thought of Rudolf Otto has shown that many of Levinas' sweeping statements about Judaism are somewhat simplistic and one-sided compared to a more detailed study of religious experience. The opening up of the realm of the numinous immediately limits and renders relative the very importance of ethics — upon which upon Levinas has constructed his entire religious philosophy.

Notes:

1. DL 28.
2. DL 29.
3. Edith Wyschogrod, *Emmanuel Levinas: The Problem of Ethical Metaphysics* (The Hague: Martinus Nijhoff, 1974), 164.
4. DL 29.
5. "Dialogue with Emmanuel Levinas" interview by Richard Kearney, in: *Face to Face with Levinas*, ed. Richard Cohen (Albany: State University of New York Press, 1986), 20.
6. Immanuel Kant, *Kritik der reinem Vernunft* (Berlin: Akademie Ausgabe, 1910), 6v8. The Kant quotations to follow are all taken from the Akademie Ausgabe, (1910) Abbreviations: KrV - *Kritik der reinen Vernunft*; KpV - *Kritik der praktischen Vernunft*; KdUK - *Kritik der Urteilskraft*; Rel - *Die Religion innerhalb der Grenzen der blossen Vernunft*.
7. KrV b xxx.
8. KpV v, 224.
9. KpV v, 125.
10. KdUK v, 137.
11. KdUK v, 134.
12. KdUK v, 129.
13. Rel I, 145.
14. Friedrich Schleiermacher, *On Religion*, trans. John Oman (New York: 1958), ix.
15. Ibid., 35.
16. Frederick Copleston, *A History of Philosophy*, vol. 7, Part I (Garden City, New York: Image Books, 1965), 144.
17. Ibid.
18. Schleiermacher, 31.
19. Mircea Eliade, *Myths, Dreams, & Mysteries*, trans. Philip Mairet (Great Britain: Collins, 1974), 123.
20. Rudolf Otto, *The Idea of the Holy*, trans. John W. Harvey (London: Oxford University Press, 1980), 1.
21. Ibid., 2.
22. Ibid.
23. Ibid., 6.
24. Ibid.
25. Ibid., 10.

[26] Ibid., 12.
[27] Ibid., 14.
[28] Ibid., 19.
[29] Ibid., 20.
[30] Ibid., 51.
[31] Ibid., 56.
[32] Ibid., 29.
[33] Eliade, 124.
[34] Otto, 109.
[35] Ibid.,110.
[36] Ibid.,111.
[37] Ibid.,140.
[38] Ibid., 141.
[39] Ibid.

11
Rosenzweig and Buber

Franz Rosenzweig (1886 - 1929) and Martin Buber (1878 - 1965) have had a very large influence, not only on Emmanuel Levinas, but on twentieth century philosophy and theology. The better known of the two, Martin Buber, needs no introduction: like Mahatma Ghandi or Albert Schweitzer, he was the conscience of an age. His works are now classics, their influence reaching beyond philosophy and theology to psychology and education. Franz Rosenzweig, though less renowned than Martin Buber, has influenced twentieth century Jewish thought and Jewish theology more than anyone else. Levinas has said that in his own writings Franz Rosenzweig is too often present to be quoted. Furthermore, Levinas is convinced that Rosenzweig has had a much greater influence on non-Jewish German philosophers than they are willing to admit — despite the fact that they never quote him.

The primary concern of Franz Rosenzweig and Martin Buber is the fate of the individual. Rosenzweig attacks idealism for its subordination of the individual to the all-embracing, abstract whole, what Levinas later calls the "totality." Martin Buber is the prophetic voice that calls men to moral responsibility. Bernard Martin, in his book *Great Twentieth Century Jewish Philosophers* writes:

> Buber reacts to the dehumanization of man and the destruction of authentic personal relations wrought by the technological, objectifying orientation of contemporary civilization with a passionate plea for a return to the life of dialogue in which persons as such are confirmed in their nobleness and uniqueness" [a theme which Levinas echoes over and over in his "sousie de l'autre"][1.1]

Franz Rosenzweig and Martin Buber had a common teacher in Hermann Cohen (1842 - 1918). Cohen is the first twentieth-century Jewish philosopher, though distinctly a product of the preceding century, in which his entire formation took place. He initiated some of the major trends in twentieth-century philosophy of religion: the notion of "the living God"; the use of religious convictions as sources of reference in philosophy; and the "I - Thou" dialogical relationship between individuals. Certainly Levinas was also influenced by Cohen.

Cohen, "the last of the Kantians," only became interested in Judaism toward the end of his life, when he began writing works such as *The Concept of Religion in the System of Philosophy*. Until this time, God had been a mere idea for Cohen — the God of the philosophers: Any kind of relationship with a living God was out of the question. God had to be within a system of knowledge. In *Ethics of Pure Will* (1904) Cohen writes: 'God must not become the content of belief if that belief is to mean something distinct from knowledge.' For Cohen as for Kant, God was simply the idea of truth. In Kantian thinking, an idea in itself could not be linked with the concept of existence: it was only an instrumental necessity, something introduced into the structure of ethical thoughts in order to establish a unity between nature and morality.

Later, changes in Cohen's thought take place: he begins to write such things as 'the love of God is the love of religion. The love of God is therefore the knowledge of morality.' God now becomes more real; He becomes the object of love. Cohen has begun to equate religion with morality.

In *The Concept of Religion in the System of Philosophy*, the use of religion in philosophy becomes legitimized by one of the strictest philosophers of the era: Cohen writes that when I love God, I no longer think Him. God is no longer a mere intellectual postulate. Cohen says the love of God exceeds all knowledge; it becomes the catalyst for my good actions toward others. Man is no longer "independent of his obligations" — they are no longer outside him, as in Kantian thought; they spring from the heart of the individual. Cohen continues saying that I cannot love God without devoting my whole heart to my fellow man, without devoting my entire soul to all the spiritual friends in the world around me. The precedence of the other person becomes a central theme for Cohen; it is treated at length in *Religion of Reason from the Sources of Judaism*.

Thus the great priority of the Other begins to take root in twentieth-century Jewish thought. For Cohen, it was no longer the ego which embarked upon a discovery of all that lay outside it; self-discovery comes *from* an outside source, *from* the Other, as in the philosophy of Levinas. Cohen writes, "only the Thou, the discovery of the Thou, is able to bring myself to the discovery of I, to the discovery of the ethical knowledge of my I." Cohen explains that my fellow man, when I first come into contact with him, is not immediately a Thou; there is a Thou that I must learn to see in him. Levinas's theme of the Other as revealer of the Infinite is already foreseen in *Religion of Reason from the Sources of Judaism*:

> The concept of the fellow man conceals a correlation of its own, namely, that of man and man, but in this narrower correlation there is merely an initial unfolding of the meaning and the context of a more universal one. For the correlation of man and God cannot be actualized if the correlation of man and man is not first included.[3]

God, the Infinite, the Absolute, the Trace of the One who has passed — whatever one chooses to call this reality — is first disclosed in the Other.

A final important thought of Cohen's also found in Levinas, is that God can only reveal Himself in a relation; and a relation can only be had with man, not with nature: "For the opinion that God also reveals himself in the world is an incorrect idea that vacillates in the direction of pantheism . . . God in no way reveals himself in something, but only to something, in relation to something. And the corresponding member of this relation can only be man."[4]

As Rosenzweig is too often present in the writings of Levinas to be quoted, so parallels with Levinas are too numerous in the following brief introductions to Rosenzweig and Buber, to be noted separately. The introductions are primarily to acquaint the reader with the Jewish philosophical milieu of the earlier part of this century, that in which Levinas was to find much inspiration.

Franz Rosenzweig is best known for his monumental work *The Star of Redemption* (1921). It is a very difficult book, in places extremely complex, written in the style of Hegel's *Phenomenology of the Spirit*. Rosenzweig wrote most of the *Star of Redemption* during World War I, on postcards, which he would send to his mother who collected them for him. *The Star of*

Redemption contains practically all of Rosenzweig's thought, for he became terminally ill soon afterwards and died eight years later, at the age of forty three. One of Rosenzweig's purposes in writing *The Star of Redemption* was to prepare a guide for marginal Jews desiring to reappropriate their religious heritage.

Judaism was not teaching for Rosenzweig, it was an event of being. Levinas writes of Rosenzweig, "For me he was the first Jew to rise above all the 'ghetto' complexes. His Judaism was neither morose nor disturbing, nor the result of some kind of piety. His Judaism was free and virile, comforting and beautiful."[5] In *The Star of Redemption*, Rosenzweig describes his philosophy as being diametrically opposed to the entire Western philosophic tradition, inaugurated by Thales in the 6th century B.C. and finding its culmination in Hegel. Thales' "all is water" became the monistic prototype of philosophical truth. For Rosenzweig, this denied the truth of everyday experience. The search for the "essence of things" which began with Thales' popular quote was a reduction of the plurality of reality to one universal truth contained within a Great All. Everything from then on became reducible: for the ancients, everything was reduced to the world; for medieval theology, to man.

This last, Idealism, posited a unity of being, and, as being in idealism is based on thought, a unity of thought as well, capable of comprehending all being. Rosenzweig rebelled against such fundamental principles. God, man, and world are separate, irreducible entities given in experience; they are not the result or product of thought. Thought can but accept them as given, and seek to understand them. Idealism also denies the reality of particular men in favor of "man in general," and particular consciousness in favor of consciousness in general. Furthermore, it tries to console man, to remove his fear of death. But man does not want to escape the fetters of existence. And man abhors theories which deny his individuality.

In *Das Büchlein vom gesunden und kranken Menschen* (The Little Book of the Healthy and Sick Man), Rosenzweig presents an idealist who becomes cured from his mental paralysis by discovering "The New Thinking," based on common sense, or healthy, uncorrupted thinking. Man must verify things for himself, focus on life and not on ideas, come to his own truths; in the words of St. Paul, "try everything, retain that which is good." There may be one universal truth but it is only such for God — human truth must be manifold. What is made true is verified by the individual; he already has within himself the necessary materials — given to him through revelation — to form a bridge between "objective truth" and his own "subjective truths."

Influenced by Cohen's *Religion of Reason from the Sources of Judaism*, Rosenzweig developed his concept of *Sprachdenken* (speech thinking): Speech is distinguished from logical or grammatical thinking. In logical thinking, the thinker has no genuine partner; he speaks to no one but himself: "it is not speaking, that is, it is not 'silent' speaking but rather a speech prior to speaking, the secret formation of speaking."[6] *Sprachdenken* is dialogical. One always speaks to someone and for someone, always someone definite: real conversation with a real someone in which something unforeseen may happen. In Levinasian terminology, *Sprachdenken* is the Other — "perennially new, primordial, escaping description." Rosenzweig sees speech as miraculous; language is the fulfillment, the beginning, middle, and end of man. Speech is "truly mankind's morning gift from the Creator ... it is the seal of humanity in the now." [7] In philosophy and theology, *Sprachdenken* translates into the "common sense" of "the New Thinking." Rosenzweig was very much for the marriage between theology or religion and philosophy. The philosopher must also be a theologian:

> The true relationships of these two renewed services is a sisterly one . . . and this must lead to a personal union of their bearers. Theological problems must be translated into human terms, and human problems brought into the theological. The problem of the same God, for instance, is only a part of the logical problem of names in general; and an aesthetic that gives no thought to the question whether artists can be saved is a polite but incomplete science.[8]

The starting point of knowledge must not be in abstract thought but in something real and simple, in man in the plainest sense. Philosophy need not fear simple questions; a relation between philosophy and life does not mean the end of philosophy, but its beginning. A union with religion offers philosophy such a chance. Religion is not a reality unto itself, distinct from everyday life. It is the throb of life, long before it is confession. It is where God comes into relation with man, and man into relation with the world. Philosophy can only benefit from religion; in dealing with the questions of everyday living religion is always both anterior and posterior to philosophy.

Rosenzweig strove for a synthesis between thinking and faith, much as Levinas "philosophizes with the Bible." This synthesis does not mean that God is once again in need of new conceptualizations — on the contrary, God is beyond the conceptualizations of a philosophical system, always a surplus beyond His essence, a line of thought which Levinas was later to pursue in his *Otherwise Than Being or Beyond Essence*.

Revelation, a central theme of *The Star of Redemption*, is God's love toward man. It is not that there is first love and then revelation, nor revelation and then love: this love *is* revelation. God turns toward man in love, and man's understanding of the event is revelation. The content of revelation is nothing more and nothing less than the presence of God. Aware that He is the object of divine love, man is saved from his primordial loneliness; the isolation in which he is originally enclosed is broken. Man's answer to this divine love is his love of neighbour. The love of neighbour, in the words of Levinas, is when an I learns to say thou to a him. This is redemption:

> Life is revelation; being is relation. The world does not sustain itself as in idealism. The world isn't an idea, the world is created. It indicates toward an origin. Creation isn't the limit of being but its foundation. Things exist in relation to each other, and for each other. Even the relation of God and man is not one of two independent and distinct entities, but rather God for man and man for God.[9]

Judaism bears witness to this life of relation. Instead of legislating totalizing thought, as do philosophy and industrial society, Judaism steps outside the picture and concentrates on the attitudes of life; it remains "outside of the world." Rosenzweig says the Synagogue is unlike the Church, which mixes in worldly affairs: it is a silent monitor, unseduced by what is common to all men. The Synagogue denies the world, the Church affirms it. Rosenzweig was the first to see Judaism and Christianity as equally valid — Judah Halevi and Maimonides had understood the Church to be, like Islam, merely preparing the way for the Messiah. Judaism and Christianity equally bear witness to God, Judaism by its very existence, the Church through its missionary works, bringing God to the pagans. Judaism and Christianity are both authentic and valid expressions of one religious truth; both are paths that lead to God, and the truth of God can be verified in each. Both have indispensable roles to play in the divine economy of salvation, but neither of them is an absolute. Both are human and fallible, partial understandings of the divine truth.

Thus, there are three major themes in Rosenzweig which have had enormous influence on 20th century Jewish thought, and especially on Martin Buber, and Emmanuel Levinas; life as relation, the marriage between theology and philosophy, and the equal importance of Judaism and Christianity.

Martin Buber, like his predecessors Cohen and Rosenzweig, came to the Bible later in life. Afterwards, he was overcome by the spirit of Hasidism, though he did not become a practicing hasidic. In his youth, he had been influenced by the German philosopher of culture Wilhelm Dilthey (1833 - 1911), as well as by Nietzsche, Kierkegaard, and Dostoyevsky. From Nietzsche Buber learned to value the concrete and the immediate over the abstract and the ideal; from Kierkegaard the immediacy of the divine-human relationship and the fearfulness and insecurity of man called to exercise responsible freedom; from Dostoyevsky the psychology of the human soul. Buber discovered the presence of the divine in Hasidism. From the Hasidics, he learned that common reverence and common joy of soul are the foundations of genuine human community. Buber also valued the practical side of Hasidism, its endeavour to "hallow the everyday."

Buber presented an image of man to an age which no longer had one — an age much like our own. He showed how man is involved in a genuine dialogical relation with the world around him — with creation and with God. He spoke of an "ethics of lived life"; an ethics which carries responsibility within itself and feels obliged to respond to life. He writes of the necessity to respond to all situations of life — to respond to the look of a dog, the hand of a child, the misery of a crowd. One who does not respond, who lives in "solitude," may have ideas and thoughts, but everything will remain exterior to him. Nature for such a person is either a state of soul or an experience, a passive object of knowledge; never a partner. Nothing ever transforms itself for him "into a perceptible work of contemplation and sensitivity." One who lives dialogically, however, attempts to respond to the world around him; things become transformed for him, take on different appearances. Buber tells how his first real awareness of alterity, of the "otherness" of the world, came from his grandfather's horse:

> When I would stroke the huge mane, sometimes combed wondrously smooth and at others wondrously wild, and would feel the living live under my hand, it was as though the element of vitality itself were touching my skin, something that was not I, not I at all, unknown to the I, quite manifestly The Other...[10]

One finds many instances of these "transformations" in the phenomenology of Levinas: the face becomes more than "just a face" — a revelation; the "bonjour" is the "first miracle"; labor, rest, domicile — all become transformed and carry new meanings beyond the immediate.

Dialogical life for Buber is not a debate between egoism and altruism. It is not a moralizing subject. Neither should it be confused with love: dialogue is not love. Dialogue is when one goes "out of oneself" towards the Other. The dialogical movement is a turning toward another, when the Other becomes "present." This is not love, but love without true dialogue is diabolic.

Such was Buber's response to an era of massive depersonalization and dehumanization. Authentic human relations can only be salvaged by turning to the Other as Thou, making the Other present in his concrete wholeness and uniqueness. Man fully becomes himself only between man and man; in *das Zwischenmenschliche* (the inter-human). Thou is a radical alterity, and the I - Thou relationship is one of radical responsibility, one of decision, direction and trust. In *The Eclipse of God*, Buber writes:

> My soul does not and cannot include the Other, and yet can nevertheless approach the Other in this most real contract. This Other, what is more, is and remains over and against the self, no matter what completeness the self may attain, as the Other . . . Only then, when, having become aware of the unincludable otherness of a being, I renounce all claim to incorporating it in any way within me, or making it a part of my soul, does it truly become Thou for me. This holds for God as for man.[11]

Alongside the I - Thou relationship exists the I - It relationship, which is when the Other becomes merely the object of knowledge, something for my experience, use, enjoyment, or control. Saying Thou is not an experiencing of the Other; experience is a distancing from Thou. In certain contexts, I - It relationships can be legitimate, as in the natural sciences. But Buber saw the I - It relationship growing way out of proportion. He saw man in the twentieth century coming under the sway of "pan-technical mania" — the unchecked growth of the I - It attitude.

In the philosophy of Martin Buber, God is the wholly other, and the fully immanent. The perfect relation is to see all things in God and this all-pervading presence "revealed" in the Thou. This does not mean that God can be "shown," nor is it intended to be a proof of His existence. The Thou is where testimony is given to the existence of God, much like the Other in Levinas: 'One doesn't find God if one leaves the world and one doesn't find God if one stays in the world. He finds God who gives himself fully to the Thou.' Elsewhere, Buber writes: 'Every individual Thou opens a perspective on the eternal Thou.' It is not in looking for God that you will find Him, but in sanctifying the world, in giving meaning to the world and seeing it as a part of God's creation; 'to look away from the world, or to stare at it, does not help a man to reach God; but he who sees the world in Him stands in His presence. 'Here world, there God' is the language of it. For Buber as for Cohen and Rosenzweig, the true God is the living God. Religion is a holding fast to Him, not to an image that one has made of "God over there," nor even to the faith in God that one has conceived.

Buber realizes that the concept of a living God cannot be combined with rationality; for him philosophy, through intellectual reflection, has led to the intellectual letting go of God. In *The Eclipse of God* Buber explains that God has become unreal to man today — that, as the title of the book suggests, God has been eclipsed. This is the fault of philosophy, where God has become the object from which all other objects are derived. When God becomes "the Unlimited" or "Being," He is no longer the personal, living God; a barrier is erected between man and God. Eventually this leads to a refutation of the concept of the Absolute. Philosophy has finished by annihilating the Absolute; "there now exists only a product of human individuals called spirit, a product which they contain and secrete like mucus and urine."[12] Philosophy in its blindness does not even see what has happened, but still maintains that it can find God:

> An eclipse of the sun is something that occurs between the sun and our eyes, not in the sun itself. Nor does philosophy consider us blind to God. Philosophy holds that we lack today only the spiritual orientation which can make possible a reappearance of God and the gods (Hölderlin), a new procession of sublime images."[13]

Many of the "spiritual orientations" of his time were for Buber nothing more than gnosis and gnostic speculation — occult, magic, Jungian collective consciousness. These things and not atheism annihilate God. The only real God is the living God of religion: "The real God is not the product of intellectualization but is to be loved and feared, for, to begin with, He is "dreadful and incomprehensible."

Though Buber was overcome by the spirit of Hasidism, his two major works *Ich und Du* (I and Thou) and *Zwiesprache* (Dialogue) contain hardly a word about the Bible or Hasidism. It is not by chance that Buber avoids speaking of them: he set himself the task of purifying Jewish doctrine of all the elements of the "fantastic" that cling to it while at the same time preserving all the power and tension of Jewish speculative thought. He is clearly a forerunner to Levinas. Lev Shestov writes: "The Bible speaks constantly of miracles and Hasidism is so bound up with the legendary it is commonly believed that nothing would be left of either if they were purged of the fantastic. Buber has shown that one can be a believing Jew and a convinced Hasid without sacrificing intellect."[14] Buber wanted to expound his doctrine in the spirit of modern man using the language of modern man; to "translate the Bible into Greek."

In an interview with François Poirié,[15] Levinas says that he is very close to Martin Buber and grateful to him for having led the way in many respects. He did, though, arrive at his reflections on the alterity of the Other independently of Buber. Levinas criticizes Buber for being too spiritual,[16] and for not insisting enough on the ethical dimension in the I - Thou relation: it is too natural, it has an almost ontological status separate from ethics. The I-Thou relation is the strongest difference between Buber and Levinas: for Buber, this is a reciprocal relation — I owe to the Other and the Other owes to me; for Levinas, it is fully asymmetrical — my responsibility for the Other puts no responsibility upon him — he even has the right to make infinite claims upon me.

Notes:
[1] Bernard Martin, "Introduction," in *Great Twentieth Century Jewish Thinkers*, ed. Bernard Martin (New York: MacMillan Co., 1970), x.
[2] Hermann Cohen, *Religion of Reason out of the Sources of Judaism*, trans. Simon Kaplan (New York: Frederick Ungar Publishing Co., 1972), 15.

3 Ibid., 114.
4 Ibid., 71.
5 DL 279.
6 Franz Rosenzweig, *The Star of Redemption*, trans. William W. Hallo (New York: Holt Rinehardt & Winston, 1971), 109.
7 Ibid., 110.
8 Martin, *Great Twentieth Century Jewish Philosophers*, 138.
9 DL 265.
10 "The Horse," *Journal of Hebrew Literature* (Jerusalem: World Zionist Organization, 1966).
11 Martin Buber, *The Eclipse of God*, trans. (New Jersey: Humanities Press, 1979), 57.
12 Ibid., 125.
13 Ibid., 23.
14 Lev Shestov, *A Shestov Anthology*, ed. & trans. Bernard Martin (Athens, Ohio: Ohio University Press, 1970), 247.
15 François Poirié, *Emmanuel Lévinas: Qui êtes-vous?* (Lyon: La Manufacture, 1987), 123ff.
16 Theodore de Boer, "An Ethical Transcendental Philosophy," in *Face to Face with Levinas*, ed. Richard Cohen (Albany: State University of New York Press, 1986), 109.

12
From East to West. Levinas and Russian Thought.

In biographical sketches of Levinas the importance of the Russian classics as part of his early formation is usually dealt with in one sentence, immediately following one about the Hebrew Bible. Then the long list of comparisons with Husserl, Heidegger and other Western thinkers begins. Two immense heritages, one cultural, the other religious, are mentioned in passing, as if Levinas really began to think only when he first read Husserl. This is like teaching the History of Philosophy by beginning with Bertrand Russell, after a few short words about Plato and Aristotle: academic orientation is important, but seldom as much as the cultural milieu from which an author comes, and the Weltanschauung given to him in childhood. Levinas did read the Russian classics early in life, but more importantly, he comes from the cultural context in which they were written: he grew up in Tsarist Lithuania, and went to high school in Kharkov. Holy Mother Russia is no foreign concept to him — it is the fertile ground on which he was nurtured.

Which plays the greater role in a writer's intellectual formation, his religious or his cultural heritage? In the case of Levinas the two blend together; Judaism and Russian thought parallel each other in a unique way — both have a messianic consciousness. Nicolas Berdyaev, in *The Russian Idea*, writes: "Messianic consciousness is more characteristic of the Russians than of any other people except the Jews. It runs all through Russian history right down to its communist period."[1]

Russian messianic consciousness dates back to the fall of the Orthodox Byzantine Empire. In the Orthodox world, Rome was seen as corrupt; true teaching was guarded in Constantinople, the "second Rome." When the Byzantine Empire fell to the Muslims, the Moscow Tsardom was left as the only Orthodox realm. In the words of the Russian monk Philotheus:

> The Russian Tsar is the only Christian Tsar in the whole earth. In the God-fearing city of Moscow the Church of the Most Holy Mother of God stands as the representative of the Ecumenical and Apostolic Throne, it shines with light side by side with Rome and Constantinople, it is unique in the whole ecumenical world and shines brighter than the sun.[2]

Moscow became the third Rome. Her people regarded themselves as a chosen people. As with Judaism, Russia became a point of orientation, a light for the rest of the world. The Russian people saw themselves as the only true carriers of Christianity and giving witness to the true God. The entire Russian Empire took upon itself a religious vocation, which was linked with the power and transcendent majesty of the Russian State. The Russian tsar became a tsar above all other tsars, and began to trace his lineage back to Augustus Caesar. Ivan the Terrible traced his lineage back to Nebuchadnezzar. One historian of the period went even further, showing Rurik, the founder of the Russian State, to be a direct descendent of Adam. As well as the interests of the state, the tsar had to care for the salvation of souls. Of this Ivan the Terrible was particularly conscious, freeing Russia from the yoke of Tartar infidels. These manifestations of early Russian religious zeal gradually began to wane after the reforms of Peter the Great in the eighteenth century, but many of the basic ideals remained. One was a sort of sacred aura surrounding the state. This knew unmatched levels of enthusiasm after the October revolution. Another manifestation, more important for our purpose, was the concern for the salvation of mankind. This expressed itself in the nineteenth century as social and moral consciousness.

This is the originality of Russian thought — the immediate concern for the Other, for the "Humiliated and the Oppressed." Russian philosophy is not historicocentric, but anthropocentric:

> The great Russian writers of the nineteenth century created not from the joy of creative abundance, but from a thirst for the salvation of the people, of humanity and the whole world, from unhappiness and suffering, from the injustice and slavery of man.[3]

Russian literature has more of a moral and religious character than any other literature in the world. For Dostoyevsky, the Russians were a God-bearing people to whom belonged a sensitivity toward the whole world. Levinas's the 'one carrying the sins of the Other' is taken from Dostoyevsky — but Dostoyevsky is more radical than Levinas. Dostoyevsky did not believe in the existence of ordinary goodness in people. Goodness and responsibility have to have a source, and that source is suffering. Through suffering people become good and responsible.

The Russian intelligentsia was never 'bourgeois,' and neither was Russia itself. Russia cannot be bourgeois because Russians are maximalists — totalitarians, socialists, or theocrats. It is precisely that which looks like a utopia that is most realistic to Russians. Russian thought was always concerned with the transformation of the actual state of affairs. Remnants of this exist today in Soviet ideology, though twisted from the original religious context.

In Russian thought the moral element predominated over the metaphysical. Russian philosophers were not interested in creating ontologies: they wanted to transform the world. A philosopher of the turn of the century, Federov, who was to influence the poet Mayakovsky, was a searcher of universal salvation for all. For Federov, each person is answerable for the whole world and for all men, and every person is to strive for the salvation of all men and of everything. This we find in Dostoyevsky and in Levinas; Federov, however, goes further, and this was the part of his teaching that fascinated Mayakovsky: Federov believed that Christian faith must be combined with science and technology, that resurrection from the dead ought not to be solely a Christian task, but one for science as well.

The Russian intelligentsia never set itself over against the people. Snobbery and disdain for the lower classes did not exist to the degree it did in the West. On the contrary, the intelligentsia was conscious of a feeling of guilt before the people. Levinas's "we are responsible for the sins committed by others" would have needed no explanation in nineteenth century Russia, nor would it have met with any opposition.

Inwardness — 'interiority' in the language of Levinas is not an essential part only of Judaism; it is also a Russian concept. The Slavophils sought in history and culture the same kind of spiritual integrity they found in the soul. The conflict between religious consciousness and Western society, to which Levinas alludes, was a popular theme in nineteenth century Russia: the Russians, a century before Levinas, saw Western society lacking in inwardness. Ivan Kireevsky, in an essay entitled *On the Character Of*

Enlightenment in Europe and its Relation to Enlightenment in Russia, explains that in the West everything has arisen from the triumph of formal reason. This tendency to rationalistic segmentation was the "second fall" of man. The Roman Catholic Church, the ancient Roman culture, and political government arising from the violence of conquest — three elements belonging the the West — were entirely alien in Russia. Kireevsky writes that theology in the West also took on a character of rational abstraction; Orthodoxy preserved the inward integrity of spirit. The Slavophils regarded Western rationalism as the source of all evil, a form of violent, spiritual totalitarianism. K. Aksakov, another Slavophil, taught:

> In the West they kill souls and replace them by the perfecting of political forms and the establishment of good order and by police action. Conscience is replaced by law, regulations become a substitute for inward impulse, even charity is turned into a mechanical business. All anxiety is for political reforms.

Levinas's distrust of politics, then, is not surprising.

The Slavophil approach to history is not a description of actual historical events; like the Jews, they saw themselves describing spiritual orientations outside the 'rush of history.' Western Christianity is historical Christianity. Russian Christianity is not: it is an expectant Christianity, eschatological, directed towards a created world. The Slavophils sought to introduce into history timeless transcendent elements by which people could direct their lives.

The importance of community, central in Judaism, is also a Russian idea. It is the Russian choric principle, the unity of man in love and freedom. The community of the people is quite different from the individualistic chivalry of the West — not "I think," but "we think." The Russians were less socialized than the West, but they were more community conscious, more ready for a life in common. Capital punishment did not exist in Russia. The idea of execution repelled the Russians, especially the Western idea of public executions, where people looked on as if at a show. Turgeniev, witnessing an execution in Paris, had the impression that 'Nobody was looking on as a human being or as one who was conscious of being present at the carrying out of a measure of public justice. Everyone was trying to rid himself of responsibility for that murder.'

If there is one idea that dominated Russian intellectual history in the nineteenth century it would have to be that of "sobornost," as developed by Alexei Khomyakov. Sobornost was a vision of Russia as a spiritual community. The word is derived from the root "sobirat" — to bring together. In the Slavonic text of the Nicene Creed it means "catholic" — not in the sense of universality, but in the sense of bringing all men together. Sobornost was the dream of Russian Orthodox theologians; it meant the fellowship of man in unity, mutual love and freedom, rather than by regimentation and coercion. Sobornost is why subsequent Marxist theories found such fertile ground in Russia: Russian Orthodox intellectuals, opposed to authoritarianism and individuality alike, mistakenly saw Marxism as a practical means of making sobornost a reality. Sobornost may also be translated as harmony and unanimity, and in Levinas it finds its parallel in "sociality," the element of Levinas's thought most responsible for the popularity he now enjoys among the theologians of liberation.[4]

Although nineteenth-century Russian philosophical thought was preeminently religious, ethical and social in character, it should not be confused with humanism. Russian thought is humane, not humanist. European humanism had no knowledge of the problem of eschatology and was untroubled by it; the quest for the Kingdom of God upon earth was a Russian quest. European humanism was only interested in the immediate. It did not look beyond, toward a promised future, as in Judaic and Russian messianism. Russian thought saw no humaneness separate from God and the teaching of the 'end of things to come.' For Dostoyevsky, humaneness separated form God leads to inhumaneness.

Russia was also different from Europe in its atheism: Russian atheism was not born of a pride in man and his rationalist powers of explication and achievement; it was born of suffering, of compassion, of the impossibility of enduring evil in the world, in history and in civilized society. Nietzsche was greatly admired in Russia and had a large following, not for his aristocratic cultural themes or his will to power, but for his religious themes. In Russia Nietzsche was accepted as a mystic and a prophet. Religion and philosophy were always inseparable in Russia and all intellectual movements in Russia had a religious character. The socialist thinker Belinsky said that people are so stupid it is necessary to bring them to happiness by force, a theme developed in Dostoyevsky's "The Grand Inquisitor."

The concepts of guilt and sin, too, were always present among Russian thinkers. Just as medieval Christian asceticism thought it necessary to fight against individual sin, Russian revolutionaries thought it necessary to fight against social sin. Tolstoy admired Rousseau but was himself more profound and more radical than the latter, because he had the typical Russian consciousness of guilt, of which there is none in Rousseau. The great thinkers of the West did not think of such things. For this reason it is questionable whether the weight and importance of Levinas's message will ever be grasped in the Western world.

Levinas's "feeling of responsibility for the Other" and his "sentiment de coupabilité" (feeling of guilt) felt by the self toward the Other are not only Judaic, but Eastern European, and quite Russian. Levinas's asymmetrical relation with the Other is something that Martin Buber could not understand; Buber, for all his Jewish devotion, was still a Westerner. When Levinas writes about freedom as a burden, as obligation, something we would be ashamed of should we consider the havoc we cause with it, this is pure Tolstoy. For Tolstoy, it is not man who demands freedom from God but God who demands it from man.

Even Russian nihilists were religious. They were unlike Western nihilists. Western nihilism was the product of refinement. In Russian nihilism there is no refinement at all: Russian nihilists disdained refinement, culture and rhetoric. Rhetoric is not natural to Russians. It played no part in the Russian revolution as it did in the French. Russian nihilists were seekers of truth who had become disillusioned by historical Christianity and spirituality.

The best of Russian philosophy was not academic. Whenever Russian philosophers tried to be academic they did not distinguish themselves by any particular originality: they would follow in the footsteps of the German idealists. The philosopher Stankevich wrote, 'I have no desire to live in the world unless I find happiness in Hegel.' The originality of Russian philosophy lies in its having developed outside an academic framework. The Russians were incapable of remaining abstract for very long. The most systematic of Russian philosophers, Vladimir Soloviev, was a rationalist by day and a mystic by night, as the posthumous publication of his poetry revealed: he hid his private life in his systematic philosophy. Sooner or later Russian philosophers wanted to get down to the practical questions of religion, ethics and society. They enjoyed giving themselves to causes as fully as possible. Vyacheslav Ivanov, the most renowned Hellenist in Russia and a brilliant writer, a man of extraordinary learning and culture, is a colourful example: in the course of his quest for truth he was a conservative, a mystic, an anarchist, an Orthodox, an occultist, a patriot, a communist, and finally a Catholic and fascist in Rome, where he ended his life. Levinas's insistence upon the practical exigency of philosophy reflects this Russian tradition.

The Russians created an original religious philosophy, without the strict division between theology and philosophy of the West, where theologians mistrusted philosophers and philosophers considered themselves more intellectually enlightened than short-sighted dogmatic theologians. In Russia theology and philosophy went together: philosophy depended upon religion and all philosophy was religious. Russian philosophers, like the Slavophils, searched for the 'integral human spirit' without which there could be no real philosophical apprehension; Western rationalism was too makepiece and incomplete. Russian philosophers did not make the distinction between revealed theology and natural theology which was so important in the West — Russian thinking was too integral for that. Levinas refrains from making such distinctions; not so Franz Rosenzweig. Similarly, Russian Orthodoxy allowed for a greater liberty of thought than Roman Catholicism, despite the reputation of the latter for intellectualism and scholasticism, and was less juridical than Protestantism. Russia's leading nineteenth century theologian, Alexei Khomyakov, was a retired officer of the cavalry; Russia's leading twentieth century theologian was Sergei Bulgakov, a former Marxist and professor of economics. This spirit of unity between philosophy and theology continues in the works of Levinas.

Levinas's reflections on the Other as disclosing the divine resemble Soloviev's teaching on God-Manhood. Revelation is impossible in pure abstract transcendentalism; God-Manhood is the belief in the possibility of revelation in man. It was Soloviev's way of overcoming the self-sufficiency of man in humanism: revelation taking place in man has also to take place in the collectivity of mankind, in human society. Soloviev developed this line of thought into a teaching of social and cosmic utopia. Christianity was to be made actual in society, not only in the individual soul; the Kingdom of God was to be realized on earth. Soloviev's entire teaching was permeated with messianism, orientated towards the future and a harmonious 'utopian' society. Soloviev introduced the prophetic element into

Christianity and philosophy, a theme which is now popular in the theology of liberation.

Dostoyevsky said that 'all Russians are nihilists.' Berdyaev went one further, saying that "all Russians are nihilists and apocalyptics." In this chapter we have looked at the ways in which Russian thought parallels Judaism, the most predominant being the messianic expectation. When messianism becomes the basis of a philosopher's reasoning, it is difficult for him to remain 'academic.' The human mind and spirit, which strive towards a world to come, are incompatible with the academic, organized character of Western thinking. The West dislikes eschatological thought and discards it as either romantic or reactionary, depending on the message. The dislike, however, is really for fear of dangerous innovation: eschatology is too radical, most often anarchic; its teaching usually shakes the foundations of bourgeois society. Judaism is eschatological, a waiting for the Messiah, and so, originally, was Christianity: a revelation of the end of this world, a revelation of the Kingdom of God. Russian Christianity has maintained this eschatological expectation and messianic hope much more than has Western Christianity. For Russians the messianic idea of the Kingdom of God came to mean the Kingdom of Right. When Russians begin to philosophize, their reflections turn to the state of perfect existence which ought to arrive and eliminate evil and injustice in the world. They think about a world where men's actions will be guided by a consideration for fellow men, and where each is responsible for every other; for the Russian religious mind individual salvation is impossible — salvation is corporate, all are answerable for all.

We do not make the claim that Levinas studied the History of Russian Philosophy and consciously modelled his thinking upon it — he did not have to: it is the intellectual climate in which he grew up and went to school. Consciously or not, he is very much within this tradition. Whether we classify Levinas as a religious or Jewish thinker, or as a 'phenomenologist,' much of his originality for philosophy today stems from his East European heritage.

Notes:
1. Nicolas Berdyaev, *The Russian Idea*, trans. R.M. French (London: The Centenary Press, 1947), 8. Many of the ideas in this chapter are from Berdyaev's book.
2. Ibid.
3. Ibid., 25.
4. See; E. Dussel, *Histoire et théologie de la libération* Paris: Les éditions ouvrières, 1974), 6, 9-14, 147-48, 157-161, 165-66.

Conclusion

Levinas has launched an attack on Western philosophy which he calls a 'totalitizing ontology.' In his writings, when he speaks of totalization within the Western philosophical tradition it sometimes seems that he is equating all of Western philosophy with that of Hegel. Although this is not exactly the case, it is true that Levinas tends to see Western ontology as an ontology which is a comprehensive, hence totalizing grasp of beings. For him this has always been the main project of Western ontology and he sees this main current of ontology in the West as culminating in Hegel.

The Greeks, according to Levinas, established a philosophy of totality by giving primacy to reason and unity.[1] What distinguished Socratic man was his faculty of logic. He set out to reduce the multiplicity and contingency of being to the universal and necessary laws of logic. Philosophy 'totalizes' in that it reduces all Otherness to its own schemas and categories. The result is that the mystery of being is "tamed and fettered by the mind." Man is no longer seen as a partner in dialogue with the Infinite because the Infinite is reduced to the domain of logical jurisdiction and is 'determined' and 'categorized' accordingly. Dialogue becomes monologue, man talking to himself.

Furthermore, according to Levinas, Western thinking has often equated ontology with egology, the supreme maxim of which is "know thyself." Truth is reduced to the totality of the knower, and is not revealed to us through the Other, as Levinas has attempted to show in his phenomenological investigations of the other person. Once again, as with Ulysses, truth begins and ends in the Ithaca of the Self, (its goal being to return to where it began). In this egological "Vorgehensweise" freedom has become negative, meaning freedom from Otherness. Otherness represents a threat to the supremacy of the Self.

Nevertheless Levinas has no intention to discard all of Western philosophy. He also finds a thematics of infinity in Western thought, in Plato, in all metaphysics, Descartes and others. This thematics of infinity represents a peripheral theme in Western philosophy in which man is still in discourse with the Gods, that is to say, one in which he places the Good or God above being, ethics and religion higher than ontology. It is a peripheral theme in which man still admits the exteriority and transcendence of the Other.

What is the value or legitimacy of Levinas's criticism of Western philosophy? This accusation sounds very daring if not outrageous, and we must ask ourselves how successful Levinas is in backing it up. At no point does Levinas give a systematic criticism of Western ontology from beginning to end in reference to his accusation that it is totalizing; he usually mentions only certain elements of Western ontology, and often does so in a very general manner. Why does he not give a systematic criticism?

Perhaps there are two reasons; first of all, to do so would be a monumental task and secondly he is just not interested in doing so. Derrida has commented that Levinas's primary concern has been to state his philosophical vision, his investigation of which is by no means complete.

Whether or not his investigation is complete, his accusation that Western philosophy has committed such a grand transgression is not backed up with a sufficient explanation nor is there a sufficient number of examples given.

Not only does Levinas lack philosophical rigour on this part, but the very existence of such a 'black hole' in his theory leads the reader to third possible reason for his lack of detailed criticism. Perhaps a sufficient explanation or a sufficient number of examples is not possible because the accusation itself is unfounded, or exaggerated.

This is a major problem with Levinas. Levinas's criticism of Western philosophy is based almost entirely upon Hegel and Heidegger. It is true that his critique of Heidegger is a very thorough one, but Heidegger is not all of Western philosophy. Normally in philosophy one proves or disproves (if one is of the conviction that there are no proofs in philosophy, makes acceptable or unacceptable) a certain position by offering sufficient evidence to support one's argument. Ironically, reading Levinas we find that he comes up with more examples of infinity in the Western philosophical tradition (he mentions Plato, Descartes, Kierkegaard, Bergson) than of totality (for which he usually mentions only Hegel or Heidegger). That he mentions Descartes as a supporter of the infinity theme in Western philosophy is particularly ironic since it is Descartes who was responsible for bringing the measure of subjectivity (the former 'entelecheia' of the Greeks) down from its transcendental 'exterior' throne and placing it within the Ego. Levinas is contesting the egocentrism of Western philosophy and then using a major exponent of 'egocentrism' to back up his own contestation. This not only throws into doubt the value and legitimacy of his accusation against Western philosophy but also makes it at times incomprehensible. Very often the reader just cannot figure out what is going on any more. In the end the accusation comes across as being too simplistic and it seems that Levinas is basically doing the same thing as Heidegger, tarring everything with one brush, accusing us all of a huge collective error. This does not mean that the accusation is totally unfounded (about this more to come later) but only that it is unconvincing in its presentation and, in strict philosophical terms, unjust.

A few more contradictions in Levinas's philosophy revolve around the concept of Western philosophy. What exactly does he mean by Western philosophy? This is unclear because Levinas uses the terms 'Western philosophy,' 'Western ontology,' 'the West,' and 'Socratic man' interchangeably. Can Western philosophy be equated with ontology? Is all of philosophy in the West an ontology? Is all philosophical 'Weltanschaung' in the West Socratic? The answer is, evidently, no. Granted, when Levinas makes such equations what he has in mind is that all of the Western philosophical tradition, no matter what epoch, can be somewhere or other tucked into the great, all encompassing sack of Being. Regardless of the dubiousness of such a position, the loose usage of terms is once again too simplistic, and often confusing.

Matthew Arnold in *Culture and Anarchy* wrote:

> Hebraism and Hellenism — between these two points of influence moves our world. At one time it feels more powerfully the attraction of one of them, at another time, of the other; and it ought to be, though it never is, evenly and happily balanced between them.

This quotation from Matthew Arnold opens up another contradiction in Levinas's usage of the term Western philosophy. Levinas equates Western philosophy with a purely Hellenic tradition, but in reality we Westerners have undergone quite an evolution since the times of the Greeks.

Our Western culture is not purely Hellenic but biblical as well. Many philosophers of the Western tradition from Augustine to the Scholastics did not have a purely Hellenic point of departure in their writings, but also a biblical one; this is true of Descartes, Kant and even Hegel himself. To call Western philosophy Hellenic and thus totalizing, and to oppose it to a biblical vision of man, is contradictory since Western philosophy is in so many ways already biblical. Levinas wants to lay the principles for a new ethics upon a biblical view of justice instead of upon an ontology but so many of our Western ethical values already come from the Bible. Levinas calls Western philosophy Hellenic and totalitarian but much of our Western tradition is itself influenced by the Bible which he considers to be untotalitarian.

Another question we must ask is how much Levinas himself escapes the tradition of Western philosophy which he is protesting against? J. De Greef in his article "Ethique et Réligion chez Levinas" maintains that Levinas does not really differ all that much from other philosophers within the Western tradition. Levinas says that ethics is not a religion without God, but rather without theology, and that by means of its practical exigency and of its having put the 'reflective and thematical' process into question. "Dans mon être réligieux, je suis en verité." According to J. De Greef this means that the ego only realizes and perfects itself by way of relation to alterity, or by way of the mediation of the Other (détour médiatisant de l'Autre). In this sense that which is criticized in *Totality and Infinity* is not so much the process of reflection and thematization itself, but rather certain fundamental and historical methods of this process that are not capable of returning to their origin or arriving at their end.[2] The problem for the reader of *Totality and Infinity* is, then, to know if 'passing by way of the Other' (détour par l'autre) would in the end be none other than a return to Self (retour au Moi), having reached one's "être en vérité."

To answer the question of whether or not Levinas differs from the Western tradition one can refer back to the position of J. De Greef as mentioned above in this conclusion in which he finds that Levinas differs and does not differ, that he differs and then again cannot differ. It is obvious that Levinas differs in that he is presenting a Biblical view of man and creation instead of a Hellenic one. On the other hand he is also employing the 'fruits' of the Western tradition. He is using the language of the Greeks and of course, he invokes the idea of the infinite. In any event, Levinas whether he wants to or not, has to intertwine the two traditions, Hellenic and

Hebraic. It is a predicament which Levinas is aware of. For example in *Otherwise than Being*, he seeks to think transcendence. But in order to think transcendence, one has to think, something which is in an other way (autrement) than Being or beyond (au-délà) Being. This statement proposes a certain concept of Being; but when we say that transcendence "is," we have to ask ourselves how we can think beyond Being. It is Hebraic transcendence Levinas seeks to think while speaking in terms of Hellenic Being.

Levinas is speaking in a Hellenic language and yet at the same time is attempting to break out of its totality. Perhaps this is the reason for the vagueness of many of his expressions. As Derrida writes: "In effect, when confronted by the classical difficulties of language...Levinas cannot provide himself with the classical resources against them."[3]

The point is, Levinas cannot escape logocentric language, because it is our only philosophical language. But is he justified in attempting to derive his own language of indirection which points beyond it? Not really, but some leniency should be allowed in this domain.

On the one hand philosophers are aware of the limitations and inadequacies of language but it is questionable if one has the right to prohibit them from, at least at times, attempting to go beyond such physical boundaries. A philosopher lusts for understanding as a Christian for righteousness and therefore has the right to question, to experiment.

On the other hand, as far as adherence to philosophical rigour is concerned, Wittgenstein's "worüber man nicht reden kann, soll man schweigen" is also valid. Under the exacting observations of an analytical philosopher many of Levinas's formulations would sound like nonsense. But analytical philosophy is not all of philosophy. Simon Frank, well known in Russia before the revolution wrote; "Essentially, philosophy is not only science. Perhaps philosophy is science only in a very removed sense. In its deep-rooted essence philosophy is a suprascientific, intuitive interpretation (überwissenschaftliche intuitive Weltanschauungslehre) in a very close relationship to religious mysticism."[4] Both Wittgenstein's and Frank's principles can be applied to Levinas. Although Levinas does not adhere to Wittgenstein's principles, and therefore damages his acceptability, looking at him from Frank's position nevertheless allows to see some merit and legitimacy in his philosophical attempts, even though we see that he should have striven for more of a balance between the two.

Finally, Levinas has attempted to found philosophically what is essentially a religious insight, i.e. infinity. Inspired by Descartes' "Idea of the Infinite" wherein the "ideatum" surpasses the "idea," he has attempted to found infinity on a phenomenological investigation of the "infinitesimal opening" disclosed to us in the other person. As mentioned in chapter three, we have to deal with another kind of intentionality which is directed toward that which it cannot grasp and which, because it cannot be grasped, verges more on religious insight rather than on purely philosophical speculation.

Therefore, perhaps light could be shed upon the concept of totality as developed by Levinas by examining it from the perspective of religious intuition rather from purely philosophical constation. The ego-centric, possessive, all encompassing, all subsuming totalizing tendency of reason which craves for omniscience and omnipotence, very closely parallels the biblical story of the fallen state of man. Religious language calls this egocentrism original sin. So if this brutally indifferent totalitizing tendency keeps creeping into man's faculty of reason throughout history this does not necessarily mean that his faculty of reason or any of the philosophical precepts which he has inherited are in themselves to blame for it. This does not mean that Western philosophy itself, in its analytical and conceptual structures, is totalitarian or fosters totalitarianism, but rather that it is man, by way of his egoistic nature, who is responsible for any conquering, totalizing tendencies which he may impose upon his mode of reasoning. In this sense, it is not Western philosophy with its love of reason which is guilty of nurturing totalitarian structures of thought (enslaving or totally annihilating others) but rather it is only Western philosophy with its highly developed process of reasoning which can restrain man from plunging headlong into such treachery. Totality, according to Levinas, is enforced dominance of the one over the other. There are two ways we can recognize this as wrong; by being taught by way of religious parable or by having the evils of it explained to us rationally, by way of reason, — the Western philosophical way, — which is precisely what Levinas has done!

What can we make of the above listed shortcomings in Levinas's claims? Do they mean that his writings should be discarded? Not really since Levinas's accusations are not totally unfounded. Much of Western philosophy *can* be interpreted in terms of totality, beginning with the Homeric quest for the Ithaca/Self, to the closed ontological systems of the

Scholastics, to the totalitarian political ideologies which exist in the world today. One of the benefits of Levinas's accusation is that he shows us that Western philosophy has not been conscious enough of the other person, has never really come to grips with the Other:

> ... Levinas seeks to correct what he considers the biased and arbitrary adherence of Western culture to autonomous Hellenic reason — a reason which judges the world without consideration of persons or personalities. The correction which Levinas proposes involves phenomenological reemphasis on the interpersonal experience as the counter balance which surpasses the limitations of Hellenic reason.[5]

To give a comprehensive final verdict on the accusations which Levinas levels against Western philosophy (if at all possible) would require a very extensive study, an investigation of all major Western philosophers with respect to this accusation which could be an enormous task. From the material which has been presented thus far, we see that Levinas's accusations are not really sufficiently substantiated.

Therefore, we propose an amendment to Levinas's position: Instead of calling Western philosophy totalitarian because of its subservience to reason and its affection for systematization we propose to say that because Western philosophy both elevates and adheres to reason, it can be prone to fall into the totalitarian 'trap.' Because of the high level of rationalization in Western philosophy there is the danger of forgetting the individual, of not seriously seeing the Other in his uniqueness, of treating him merely as a "psychic aid," a "symbol" a "pawn of ideology" or whatever else; of being oblivious to the revelation of ontological truth disclosed to us in the other which lies "beyond reason monologuing with itself." This is one of its dangers, but this does not mean that it is necessarily so.

Levinas is commonly considered to be an "important and original" thinker. In what lies his originality? Certainly it is rooted in the Eastern European culture from which he comes, and which he could not but bring with him to the West. Yet, as this book has shown, Levinas is deeply imbedded in the tradition of twentieth century philosophy, and in that of idealism as well — the greatest novelty of Levinas is in his autonomy. Levinas was in many ways 'anti-popular,' pursuing his own line of thought, regardless of the "philosophical trends" of the day. In the 1940s, when he first asked whether or not ontology were fundamental, the question was unexpected and unheard of in continental philosophy.[6] While moral philosophy was slipping ever more rapidly into a confused state, ever having come to be seen in some circles as unnecessary; Levinas was formulating his ideas about the supremacy of the Other, the self's indebtedness to him, and the importance of putting others before oneself. In an age more and more egoistical, Levinas discovered the voice of conscience in the Other. He developed a new kind of moral thinking, one which did not promote the supremacy of the will, as did rationalism or existentialism. As Shestov writes in *Potestas Clavium*, "rationalism fears and detests the extreme zones; it holds itself firmly in the middle zone, in the center around which are disposed all the points of the surface that it studies and with which it is concerned." In the radicalness of his asymmetrical relationship with the Other, Levinas progresses beyond this middle road, out of rationalism. And yet he avoids the extreme of irrational mysticism. As Maurice Blanchot writes, "the philosophy of Levinas obliges him to go beyond reason but not into the faculty of the irrational or towards a mystical effusion, but rather towards another reason, towards the other as reason or demand."[7] Levinas has avoided creating any kind of a moral system; yet, very cleverly, he has left us with a definite code of behaviour: "I am my brother's keeper." During the 1960s, when philosophers and even theologians were plunging into structuralism and 'demytholization,' Levinas was discovering the Other in Judaic legendry, writing about God and the need to respect sacred scripture, to interpret it spiritually. Through the impressiveness of his phenomenological 'baggage' he succeeded in re-opening the debate about God in philosophy: once again a philosopher can speak about God, without shame or the fear of not being taken seriously.

Closing remarks:
I had originally thought about giving this book the title "The Interiority of Exteriority." I decided however that such a title could prove to be needlessly confusing and perhaps a little too "sensational" and since the main concern of this book has been Levinas's "philosophy of religion" the present title was considered more suitable. With the entire development of the phenomena of the Other in this book, of the importance of that which is "outside of myself" beckoning and appealing to me, the concept of interiority may also prove to be confusing.

What Levinas means by 'interiority' is the irreducibility of the individual to the totality. In the exteriority of his being, in the Otherness of his existence, the Other reveals that there is more to reality than the Self and more to Otherness than his own finite and limited alterity. "The Other's ultimate revelation is of the exterior dimension of human existence — a dimension which is irreducible to thematic systematization and totalitization. He indicates the opening of the exterior to the interior."[8] Levinas lets us know that the identity of the individual does not consist in being like to itself, and in letting itself be identified from the outside by the finger that points to it; it consists in being the same — in being oneself, in identifying oneself from within.... It is true that the Other does in a certain sense, "take us outside of ourselves" but our relation with the Other is a kenotic one. The father "goes out of himself" in the son, gives himself over in the son, and yet the, father remains fully himself in the son, he has not been transformed by the son. The father remains the father and the son remains the son, yet each stands for the other in such a way that both follow their inner vocations.

> Relations such as the idea of infinity, which the formal logic of the gaze cannot let show through without absurdity, and which it prompts us to interpret in theological or psychological terms (as a miracle or as an illusion), have a place in the logic of interiority — in a sort of micrologic in which logic is pursued beyond the "tode ti." Social relations do not simply present us with a superior empirical matter, to be treated in terms of the logic of genus and species. They are the original deployment of the relationship that is no longer open to the gaze that would encompass its terms, but is accomplished from me to the Other in the face to face.[9]

This is the interiority which 'we lack' and which is awakened in Judaism's 'command to the Other.' Levinas is at no time insisting that the entire human race should embrace the Jewish faith but rather saying that the principles found in the Old Testament — the Mosaic vision of man and as presented in the Judaic tradition can (and should) be universally applied.

Such is Levinas's 'Prolegomena to any future ethics.'

Notes:
[1] Richard Kearney, "Emmanuel Levinas: On the Revelation of the Other" (Master's thesis, McGill University, 1977), 6-17.

[2] Jan de Greef, "Ethique et religion chez Lévinas," *Revue de théologie et de philosophie* 103 (1970): 38.

[3] Jacques Derrida, *Writing and Difference*, trans. Alan Bass (Chicago: University of Chicago Press, 1978), 79.

[4] Simon Frank, *Die russische Weltanschauung* (Charlottenburg: Pan-Verlag Rolf Heise, 1926), 5.

[5] Rudolph J. Gerber, "Totality and Infinity — Hebraism and Hellenism: The Experimental Ontology of Emmanuel Levinas," *Review of Existential Psychology and Psychiatry* 7 (1967): 177.

[6] Maurice Blanchot, "Our Clandestine Companion," in *Face to Face with Levinas*, ed. Richard Cohen (Albany: State University of New York Press, 1986), 43.

[7] Ibid., 42.

[8] Gerber, 186.

[9] TI 289.

Selected Bibliography

Works of Levinas:

Théorie de l'intuition dans la phénoménologie de Husserl. 4th ed. Paris: J. Vrin, 1978.

The Theory of Intuition in Husserl's Phenomenology, trans. André Orianne (Evanston, Illinois: Northwestern University Press, 1973).

De l'evasion. Montpellier: Fata Morgana, 1982.

Le temps et l'autre. Montpellier: Fata Morgana, 1979

De l'existent à l'existence. 2d ed. Paris: J. Vrin, 1981.

Existence and Existents, trans. Alphonso Lingis (The Hague: Martinus Nijhoff, 1978).

Totalité et infini. 4th ed. The Hague: Martinus Nijhoff, 1984.

Totality and Infinity, trans. Alphonso Lingis (Pittsburgh: Duquesne University Press, 1979).

Difficile liberté. Paris: Albin Michel, 1963.

Quatre lectures talmudiques. Paris: Les éditions de minuit, 1968.

Humanisme de l'autre homme. Montpellier: Fata Morgana, 1972.

Autrement qu'être ou au-delà de l'essence. The Hague: Martinus Nijhoff, 1974.

Otherwise than Being or Beyond Essence, trans. Alphonso Lingis (The Hague: Martinus Nijhoff, 1981).

Noms propres. Montpellier: Fata Morgana, 1976.

Du sacré au saint. Paris: Les éditions de minuit, 1977.

L'au-delà du verset. Paris: Les éditions de minuit, 1982.

De Dieu qui vient à l'idée. Paris: J. Vrin, 1982.

Éthique et infini. Paris: Fayard, 1982.

Ethics and Infinity, trans. Richard A. Cohen (Pittsburgh: Duquesne University Press, 1985).

Works about Levinas:

Cohen, Richard, ed. *Face to Face with Levinas*. Albany: State University of New York Press, 1986.

Derrida, Jacques, "Violence and Metaphysics," in *Writing and Difference*, trans. Alan Bass (Chicago: University of Chicago Press, 1978).

Forthomme, Bernard, *Une philosophie de la transcendence*. Paris: J. Vrin, 1984.

Guibal, Fr., *... et combien de dieux nouveaux*. Vol. 2. Paris: Les éditions Aubier Montaigne, 1980.

Kearney, Richard. "Emmanuel Levinas: On the Revelation of the Other." Master's thesis. McGill University, 1977.

Malka, Solomon, *Lire Lévinas*. Paris: Les éditions du Cerf, 1984.

Petrosino, Silvano, *La vertà nomade: Introduzione a Emmanuel Levinas*. Milan: Jaca Book, 1980.

Poirié, François, *Emmanuel Lévinas: Qui êtes-vous?* Lyon: La Manufacture, 1987.

Strasser, Stephen, *Jenseits von Sein und Zeit: Eine Einführung in Emmanuel Levinas' Philosophie*. The Hague: Martinus Nijhoff, 1978.

Wyschogrod, Edith, *Emmanuel Levinas: The Problem of Ethical Metaphysics*. The Hague: Martinus Nijhoff, 1974.

For a complete Levinas bibliography until 1981 and containing over 800 entries see:

Burrgraeve, Roger, "Emmanuel Lévinas: Une Bibliographie," *Salesianum* 39 (1977): 633-83, and 44 (1982): 459-78.

DATE DUE

FEB 0 3 2000			

HIGHSMITH #LO-45220